TWO'S COMPANY

TWO'S COMPANY

THE BEST OF COOKING FOR
COUPLES, FRIENDS & ROOMMATES

Orlando Murrin

PHOTOGRAPHY BY CLARE WINFIELD

RYLAND PETERS & SMALL
LONDON • NEW YORK

For Robert

Senior Designer Megan Smith
Art Director Leslie Harrington
Editorial Director Julia Charles
Production Manager Gordana Simakovic
Head of Production Patricia Harrington
Publisher Cindy Richards

Food Stylist Tamara Voss
Prop Stylist Polly Webb-Wilson
Indexer Hilary Bird

Published in 2021
by Ryland Peters & Small
20–21 Jockey's Fields
London WC1R 4BW
and
341 E 116th St
New York NY 10029
www.rylandpeters.com

Text © copyright Orlando Murrin 2021
Design and photographs © copyright
Ryland Peters & Small 2021

ISBN: 978-1-78879-377-3

10 9 8 7 6 5 4 3 2 1

Printed and bound in China.

CIP data from the Library of Congress
has been applied for. A CIP record
for this book is available from the
British Library.

HOW TO USE THIS BOOK

If you enjoy cooking and are looking
for fresh ideas for two, this book has
been written for you. On pages 6–13
you'll find an introduction, which
lists helpful equipment and ideas for
shopping and storage. This is the sort
of thing you might wish to read in bed.

The recipes themselves are organized
in a straightforward way, with careful
measurements and explanations. I have
assumed you know your way around
a kitchen, but in case of doubt when
I say FLOUR I mean plain/all-purpose
flour (I will specify when self-raising/
rising is necessary). BUTTER is salted.

When it comes to EGGS, food writers
have got into the habit of specifying
large eggs, when any size will do.

For the recipes in this book, I recommend
buying mixed-weight eggs – I explain
why on page 144.

Every OVEN is different, but note that
I don't generally preheat mine, and nor
need you. If this comes as a surprise,
find out why on page 9.

Dotted throughout the book are over
50 'TRICKS OF THE TRADE', which
I hope you will find of universal use in
your kitchen. If a trick catches your eye
but you subsequently can't find it, these
have their own index on page 175.

Finally, warm greetings to American
cooks, for whom we have supplied
AMERICAN MEASUREMENTS (oz.
and cups). If you are familiar with both
metric and imperial systems – stick
with one throughout a recipe, rather
than mixing and matching.

MIX
Paper from
responsible sources
FSC® C008047
www.fsc.org

Contents

Introduction

Cooking for two is an altogether different thing from family cooking or entertaining. For a start, your motivation is different – you're more likely to be doing it because you want to, in a mood of relaxation, fun and companionship. But it's also different technically: smaller quantities behave differently, cooking times diminish and processes can be skipped or streamlined. So why are we largely ignored by recipe writers? Two-person households outnumber every other kind of household – have done for decades – but most recipes still serve four, six or eight.

We are told that mental gymnastics keep the brain in shape, but it's so boring having constantly to halve or third recipes – then forgetting halfway through and trying to backtrack, or throw the lot away and start again. The alternative is to cook the whole quantity, for four (or six), and eat the leftovers up tomorrow (and the next day). How depressing it is to open the fridge in the morning and see your life stretching guiltily in front of you, like some sort of culinary penance. How wasteful in an age where there is not enough to go around to throw stuff away because you cooked too much.

If this rings a bell, I promise you that everything about this book – the dishes, the recipes, the tips – has been created expressly and exclusively for the cook-plus-one. Beyond that I have only made a couple of assumptions: that you take pleasure in the process of cooking, and are open to fresh ideas.

HOW TO USE THE RECIPES

We all cook differently. Some of us like to follow recipes to the letter, others take a freeform approach and customize recipes according to personal taste, or what's in the cupboard. I flit between the two. In writing these recipes, however, I have tried to imagine myself in your kitchen beside you, explaining step-by-step how I make the dish.

In the same way as most crafts and trades (to say nothing of DIY) begin and end with accurate measuring, I have weighed, measured and timed everything as exactly as I can, in the hope you get the same result as me. A discovery I made early during my testing operation was that when dealing with smaller quantities, it pays to apply an extra degree of care. An extra teaspoon of chilli powder will go unnoticed in a crowd-sized chilli con carne, but will blow your head off when it's just for two. Ten more minutes in the oven won't make much odds to a family-size roast, but will turn that little rack of lamb for which you paid through the nose to cinder.

Obviously, many cooks – especially experienced ones – may prefer to cook by 'feel', without buzzers going off the whole time. If this is you, please don't think me bossy. I invite you to use the recipes merely as guides, or for inspiration, and to skip over the detail.

Otherwise, I can honestly say it's all good news. Most kitchen processes get easier in direct proportion to the quantities you're dealing with. Chopping, chilling, cooking and baking all happen quicker. Egg-and-breadcrumbing – a delectable treatment for meat and fish, but a nightmare on a large scale – takes minutes, and you can whip cream for a dessert – using just a hand whisk or even a fork – in seconds. (If you buy Jersey cream, you can even do it by shaking it in the tub, before opening. Yes, it's true.) Freed from the tyranny of hungry mouths to feed, you can linger over the cooking as long as you wish, and with no polite guests to entertain, all sorts of exciting dishes that require last minute attention become possible... then you can sit straight down to enjoy them.

TWO'S GOOD COMPANY

Maybe you share the cooking, or maybe one cooks, the other clears up? Maybe you alternate? I was trained (by my mother) to clear up as I go along, and regard it almost as a point of honour that the kitchen (which is where we eat) is in good shape before we tuck in. There is no right or wrong, as long as everyone is happy.

I would, however, suggest one rule: whenever possible, avoid cooking against the clock. For years and years I cooked to a relentless timetable (it's what chefs do) and it completely spoils the pleasure. Of course, this does assume a certain easy-going patience on the part of your companion, so I think the least one can do is ensure a generous supply of tasty morsels to fill the (sometimes) waiting game until we eat. These might be as simple as bought antipasti, olives or crudités and dips, or 'themed' snacks – tortilla chips if we're eating Mexican, mini-poppadoms before an Indian meal, pretzels before hamburgers.

Wine is something else I like to delegate. Pairing food and wine so they work in harmony takes skill and forethought, and so does serving it. In this household at least, the cooking gets off to an impeccable start with a glass of something thoughtfully chosen, at just the right temperature. It turns every evening into a treat.

You will see that the recipes in this book do not include preparation and cooking times. This is deliberate – they are not designed to be cooked against the clock. A quick glance through the methods will obviously give you a good idea of how long to allow, but my philosophy is – and now always will be – it's ready when it's ready.

BATTERIE DE CUISINE

While testing the recipes for this book, I have noted what equipment is in constant use, and what gets shoved further and further back in the cupboard. I don't have much kitchen space – indeed, if I buy something new, something has to be 'sacrificed' to make room for it – but if you do, by all means treat yourself to some of today's amazing cookery gadgetry – breadmakers, Instant Pots®, rice cookers, soup machines, Thermomix®. They are all fun to use,

work superbly – and I feel slightly jealous. Back to reality, however, and here are some of the pieces of kit (beyond the obvious) which I believe make cooking for two so much easier…

- I swear by an induction hob/stovetop – it is so fast and controllable, and each burner has its own timer.
- Ovenproof saucepans: a small milk pan; a small saucepan; and a medium or large saucepan, all with lids; ovenproof frying pans/skillets, non-stick: small and large, with ovenproof lids. (If you don't have ovenproof lids, you can use foil.)
- Padded panholder – if you have ovenproof frying pans/skillets and put them in the oven (as I frequently do), this will save you many a nasty burn.
- Small and medium non-stick roasting tins and pans; baking trays and sheets – the more the merrier.
- Selection of small and medium ovenproof gratin dishes, oval, square, rectangular.
- Small food processor (not the mini-choppers designed for herbs). If you like your soups super-smooth, you can't, however, beat a (full-size) blender. I am no fan of stick/immersion blenders (I've had to repaint the ceiling too many times) but I know many cooks are, and the powerful ones do a good job.
- Instant digital thermometer (such as Thermapen®) – used throughout this book, and indispensable for testing when meat is cooked. My temperature recommendations reflect my preference: official food safety guidelines (which you can find online) are often higher.
- Multi-timer or timers – mine (Polder®) can count up and down at the same time.
- Stainless steel mixing bowls, large, medium, small.
- Small salad spinner.
- Spatulas and mini-spatulas – in abundance, for folding, scooping and transferring small quantities. Some kept separate for sweet dishes.
- Mini-whisks (also known as Wonder Whisks or Nigella Whisks) – for dressings and sauces (plus I have a rubberized version to use in non-stick pans and a plastic one that can go in the microwave).

- Electric spice grinder or designated coffee mill, to grind spices and dried herbs.
- Fat-separating jug/pitcher, especially if, like me, you love braising meat (see Trick of the Trade page 148).
- Large and small measuring jugs/pitchers (large can double-up for proving bread dough, and whisking/whipping egg whites and cream).
- Measuring spoons – one set clipped together, the other loose, to grab and go. For liquids, a level tablespoon (tbsp) is 15 ml, a teaspoon (tsp) is 5 ml.
- I would strongly recommend a sous-vide wand, and once you're hooked on the technique, a vacuum sealer. The sous-vide is a gadget which results in the tenderest, juiciest meat you ever will eat. It is the only way I would ever cook pork chops and steaks nowadays and this book contains a handful of recipes which use it. Invest in one – you will thank me.
- A note on aluminium foil, baking parchment, plastic film and kitchen paper towels. I never use these thoughtlessly, but they make light work of many kitchen procedures – preparing, assembling, cooking, storing. I have a corner in my kitchen where I set aside anything with potential for re-use. In some recipes, I suggest using baking parchment or foil 'for easy clean-up': these are cases which result in a horrible washing-up experience, so you decide.
- In a few recipes, I suggest 'cooking spray' as a way to prevent sticking: I am referring to the small squirty plastic bottles marketed for low-fat frying.
- If you enjoy baking, you may already be in possession of a food mixer. I only use it once in this book (Birthday Surprise, page 169). For small quantities, it is worth making sure the clearance between beater and bowl is correctly adjusted (you'll find advice online), so you're not whisking thin air. Alternatively, you can use a sturdy electric hand whisk.
- A radio or tablet, so that you can listen to something and never find yourself cooking alone.

AN IMPORTANT NOTE ABOUT OVENS

Do not preheat your oven. Yes, you heard me correctly. All the recipes in this book have been tested in a fan oven using the 'cold start' method. Put the dish in the fan oven, turn it on, then set the timer. Easy as that. Let me explain… Most electric ovens now sold are fan ovens. When these were introduced, the proud boast was 'no need to preheat', because once you turn a fan oven on, it immediately starts blowing hot air around the food. Somehow, down the years, the message got lost. Think of the terawatts of energy wasted while ovens around the world – fan or not – come up to heat. Elaine Boddy, who has emerged in recent years as one of the pre-eminent 'queens of sourdough', urges her followers to put their dough in a cold oven, then turn on the heat. As the oven heats, so does the dough. Yes, it works.

I also have a conventional oven, and – naturally – it takes longer to come up to temperature, as the hot air isn't blowing in the same way as a fan oven. For the purposes of comparison, my fan oven takes 8 minutes to reach 180°C/400°F, my conventional oven 14 minutes to reach 200°C/400°F, a gas oven 15 minutes to reach gas 6. Therefore… If you have a conventional or gas oven, put the dish in the cold oven, turn it on and set the timer, adding 6–7 minutes to the cooking time.

You may have been told – I must admit I am bored with being told – that all ovens vary and we should check frequently with an oven thermometer. (Note that an oven thermometer is different from the instant digital one I recommend on page 8: this type dips and dives as you open and close the oven door, like a runaway rollercoaster, and I find it utterly confusing.) I suggest you save your money, try one or two of my recipes to see if your timings tally with mine, and if not, adjust in future.

I have never owned an oven that bakes evenly front to back, so I invariably rotate the tray or baking dish halfway through, including for recipes we are warned will collapse, such as Yorkshire puddings and soufflés. (They don't.)

Just a handful of recipes in this book require a quick blast of oven heat or the grill/broiler to cook or brown them – in which case I indicate in good time that you will need to preheat your oven or grill.

INGREDIENTS

It's been said a million times, but do buy the best ingredients you can find and afford. The recipes in this book span the whole range from budget to luxurious, but everything goes up a notch if you start with the best you can.

During recent years, many artisan butchers, fishmongers, delicatessens, farmers' markets and greengrocers have thrived, and deservedly. I urge you to buy local, and in season, as much as possible. One great advantage of shopping in independents and markets is that you can buy exactly how much you need, without being saddled by family-size packs or uniform-sized products. That being said, supermarkets do a great job, and I have tried to design the recipes in this book around what is readily available, in standard pack sizes.

I have the good fortune to live in Devon, regarded by many as the dairy of the United Kingdom, so do not be surprised that many dishes in this book major on good things such as cheese, cream and butter. When I can, I buy these from the people who make them. It's common sense.

If you're cooking dishes from faraway lands, it's tempting to cut corners, and substitute something you already have for something 'authentic'. I know the feeling – it's depressing to accumulate half-used jars and bottles, used just once to try out a new recipe. Cooking with new ingredients and flavours is, however, how we develop as cooks, and – more important – seeking out 'the real thing' shows respect to the cuisines we are working with, their heritage and those who have 'curated' them, sometimes down many centuries. I try not to force this issue – the recipes in this book are designed to be mainstream and accessible – but I urge you to be open to culinary innovations and influences, as they come along.

Incidentally, if I do find myself with a 'half-used jar' which I am certain I no longer want, my solution is to walk a few doors down the street. My neighbour's teenage son Laurie is an ardent flavour-experimenter and jumps at the chance to try something new: the next Harold McGee, we all hope.

FRESH PRODUCE

- Most savoury recipes involve onion in some form. I find small onions (about 100–120 g/3½–4½ oz.) most useful when cooking for two. Or use ½ a large onion, and save the rest (I keep it in the fridge in the same stay-fresh plastic bag as my garlic and ginger: surprisingly, it does not make the fridge smell). Shallots, which are spicier and cook much faster, vary drastically in size, from 30–75 g/1–2¾ oz., so double-up if yours are small. Spring onions/scallions are great for adding punch – slice the white and some of the green as thinly as you can on the bias.

- You will find info about garlic, ginger and chillies/chiles in relevant recipes. Garlic is mashed (with salt), crushed (in a crusher) or sliced, as required, but it is always peeled first. Ginger is peeled, then grated or finely chopped, depending on the recipe. If your palate is spicy, chop chillies whole; otherwise, discard the ribs and seeds.

- A crisp head of celery, standing in a jug/pitcher of water in the kitchen, is irresistible for between-meal crunching. It may just be me, but I find it adds little to most cooked dishes, so use it if you have it, but you will usually find it marked 'optional'.

- Fresh herbs add a bright extra layer of flavour, and their vibrant colour brings dishes to life. (As an experiment, take a photograph of a plate of food with no green in it, then add some herbs and snap again. You will be amazed.) See Trick of the Trade on page 108 for tips on on how handle and store them.

- When it comes to eggs, I've recently learned that size isn't everything – see Trick of the Trade on page 144 and prepare to rethink your egg-buying habits.

- I always cook with salted butter.

- If I have suggested a particular cheese for a dish, feel free to vary it, particularly if you have access to local or artisan cheeses. Cheesemaking is a precious industry and deserves our support. Leftover cheese can be frozen: the texture will usually be impaired, but better than committing the crime of throwing it away. The same goes for leftover mascarpone, ricotta and mozzarella, incidentally.

STORECUPBOARD

- Where I specify 'oil' I mean rapeseed or another neutral vegetable oil. For 'olive oil' I use a good-quality extra virgin oil (but not high-end – I save that for dressings and drizzling). For the sake of authenticity, two recipes in this book call for corn oil. In many recipes, I suggest a little or a 'splash' of oil – the object being that the oil, once heated, should just cover the base of the pan. If I specify 1 tablespoon of oil, don't feel you have to bother to measure it – if the base of the pan is well covered, that is a tablespoon.
- Oil is usually heated to shimmering or just smoking before adding other ingredients. Butter is usually heated to the point where it has foamed, and the foam subsided, before adding other ingredients.
- My formula for vinaigrette is to mini-whisk mayonnaise, Dijon mustard, wine vinegar and seasoning in a jar, then very slowly whisk in ½ oil and ½ olive oil, to make an emulsion. Keeps in the fridge for a week.
- If you were a tomato, you too would taste better grown and canned under the Neapolitan sun. Choose the best you can get. Small (230-g/8-oz.) cans are more expensive but super-convenient for the smaller household, or use ½ a 400-g/14-oz. can (plus a splash of water to make up for the 30-g/1-oz. shortfall, if necessary).
- I love rice in all its forms, and it makes sense (as well as shows respect) to serve the rice appropriate to the dish in question (for instance, basmati with Indian food). An easy and elegant way to serve long-grain rice (also works for risotto rice, which has an appealing nutty flavour, and orzo – pasta-shaped rice) is in 'timbale' form (literally, 'drum-shaped'). Take 2 ramekins, about 150-ml/5-fl oz./⅔-cup capacity. Measure out ⅔ of a ramekin of rice and cook in salted boiling water or stock. Drain the rice, spoon it into the 2 buttered ramekins and keep warm on a mini baking tray or sheet, covered in foil. When ready to serve, invert 1 ramekin on each of 2 hot plates, then add meat and sauce or whatever.
- I make fresh breadcrumbs from leftover bread, but I find panko crumbs – light and crisp – much more useful. In little boxes, they are prohibitively expensive, so buy in big bags from ethnic supermarkets. Actually, get a HUGE one while you're at it.
- I am lobbying spice companies to sell spices in smaller quantities, to avoid waste. Till that happens, buy best-quality spices (such as Steenberg's and Penzey's) in the smallest amounts you can, and have an annual clear-out. If you have a spice grinder, grind your own where possible, and always grate nutmeg from fresh. Consider spice mixes – for instance, the up-and-coming Sizl brand. I have a fondness for paprika, but note that smoked comes in mild and hot forms – the latter can blast a dish off the Scoville scale if you're not expecting it.
- I have a special section in my storecupboard for condiments, including flavoured salts, Chinese, balsamic and other vinegars, Shaoxing rice wine, dark soy sauce (plus Indonesian kecap manis), Tabasco, Worcestershire and other sauces, plus mustards galore – and ketchup. New ones are always being added.
- Flour means plain (all-purpose) flour. To convert to self-raising, see Trick of the Trade on page 165.
- I use caster/superfine sugar (the golden variety, with caramel undertones), light muscovado (or light soft brown sugar), demerara/turbinado sugar and icing/confectioners' sugar (golden, if you can get it).

FRIDGE AND FREEZER

The shelves of my fridge door are where I keep my flavour 'uppers', which I use both for authentic cooking, and for experimentation. At any given time you will find gochujang, sriracha, 'nduja (pronounced en-doo-ya – a spicy fermented salami paste from Calabria), chipotle pastes, ethnic sauces (fish, hoisin, oyster, XO, BBQ), sesame oil and creamed horseradish. Always a tube of 'Bomba!' tomato purée/paste and jars of mayonnaise. Newcomers are always welcome.

The freezer can be useful for saving by-products and leftovers, but if my (much-loved) Auntie Sheila is reading this – you can take it too far, and end up with a collection of useless odds and ends. It goes without saying nothing must be allowed in unless it is labelled and – ideally – dated. Every 2 or 3 months I do a stocktake, and call everything out to Robert, who then types out a list. I enjoy seeing what he makes of some items – last time 'guanciale' came out as 'guacamole'. Beyond frozen peas, I hope you have discovered the joys of frozen sweetcorn/corn.

TRICKS OF THE TRADE

Dotted among the recipes you will find over 50 'Tricks of the Trade' – shortcuts and scraps of know-how I've picked up over the years. (You'll also find them indexed on page 175.) Here are a few extras I would like to share which have arisen mainly from working with food stylists and in professional kitchens (including my own)…

- If you are in a hurry, get everything out first – ingredients, equipment, the lot. I've done comparative timings, and it's about 20 per cent quicker, as well as minimizing mess as you crisscross the kitchen, opening and shutting cupboards. When I'm not in a hurry, I'm happy to crisscross, by the way.
- Season as you go along, then taste at the end. (I avoid tasting too often in the early stages, to avoid palate overload.) When doing this final tasting, first correct the level of salt, which enables you to detect the full flavour spectrum. When the salt is right, you are ready to make final tweaks. If it's flat, brighten and sweeten with a squeeze of lemon juice or a tiny pinch of sugar. If it's dull, consider more pepper, a pinch of crushed chilli/hot red pepper flakes, a splash of Worcestershire, or something else from your arsenal.
- I use fine sea salt for cooking, and flaky salt for finishing and at the table. Whatever you decide, stick to it, so you develop an instinct for how much to use.
- If in doubt, choose a larger pan than you think you need. Overcrowded – overflowing – pans are the mark of the amateur…
- If you are an Instagrammer, a couple of food styling tips. When arranging food in a dish, before cooking or when serving, rotate the dish to check it from two or three angles: it's surprising how elegant something can look from one direction, then you turn it around and it's an eyesore. When scattering chopped herbs,

Parmesan or whatever over a finished dish, the greater the height from which you drop, the more evenly and prettily the particles will land. (Although unfortunately, they will also land where you don't want them, including all over your worktop.)
- Cook on wood. I am not referring to charcoal and hickory chips, but your kitchen floor. Stone or tile floors are exhausting, and bad news for feet and knees. If that's what you have – well, you know for next time.

WHAT NOT TO COOK FOR TWO

I am not such a culinary evangelist as to deny that there are some things that are better not cooked for two. A roast chicken, for instance, with leftovers for a tasty chicken pie. Feats of cooking which demand a disproportionate amount of time and effort – home-made pasta, the great dishes of France (think coq au vin, bœuf bourguignon), pastilla from Morocco, a hand-raised pork pie – and dozens more. I have a special fondness for savoury tarts and quiches, but for me the minimum practical size will feed 4–6 people: miniaturized versions are laboursome and miss the point, with too much pastry to filling.

That being said, I hope this book demonstrates how many different types of recipes from all over the world *can* be scaled down successfully – and perhaps you'll find pointers and stepping stones to make it easier next time you do it for yourself. Even if you do find yourself occasionally halving an egg.

WHAT NEXT?

Most food writers would agree that although in theory we would like everyone to cook our recipes, it's scary when they do. What if it goes wrong? What if they don't like it? Occasionally, I've been invited out to eat, to find my own recipes are on the menu. It's intended to be flattering, but believe me, it's unnerving.

Despite these qualms, I believe food writers should be accountable, and I would genuinely like to know how you get on with the recipes in this book. In this day and age it's impossible to hide even if one wanted to, but feel free to contact me via the usual channels. I mean it.

WEEKNIGHT TREATS

When you're looking for something to give your evening a lift, here are some ideas to turn ordinary into special. Depending on your rhythm, some are fast, some slow, but they're all firm favourites in our household, and all completely practical for two.

Cheese baked in puff pastry

This recipe is a homage to the pasty, that parcel of goodness which Cornish wives used to slip into the pockets of their menfolk to sustain them through their hours of toil down tin mines or in the fields. Much pride is taken to this day in 'crimping' the edge to form a neat and comely finish.

My favourite cheeses for this dish are a pair of luscious cows' milk cheeses from southern England called – and yes, they sound like a variety act – Tunworth and Winslade. Once you discover these creamy marvels, it will be love at first taste. A small Camembert makes an excellent alternative. If you prefer to remove the rind – I don't – slice it away as thinly as possible. Most small round cheeses weigh in at 250 g/9 oz., so for this recipe you will need half. While you're at it, it's very little extra trouble to make a spare to put in the freezer. This can be egg-washed and baked from frozen (35–40 minutes – use a skewer to check the centre is hot). Note: the remaining pastry can be frozen or used for the Antipasti Tart, see page 48.

A crisp green salad is the perfect accompaniment. At the risk of being laughed at, I recommend Iceberg lettuce, which I find sweet, cool and crunchy, and a pleasant change from bitter salad leaves. It is also an excellent vehicle for a well-made dressing, such as my vinaigrette on page 12.

25 g/1 oz./¼ cup walnut pieces, toasted (see Trick of the Trade, page 17)

2 tbsp chutney (I like mango), onion marmalade, or a mixture

150–180-g/5½–6¼-oz. ready-rolled puff pastry (½ a pack)

½ a 250-g/9-oz. Tunworth, Winslade, Camembert, or other creamy cows' milk cheese

1 egg beaten with a little milk, to make an egg wash

a sprinkling of nigella seeds (optional)

1 Chop the toasted walnut pieces. If your chutney is on the chunky side, chop it up a bit, too.

2 If necessary, lightly roll the pastry to about 25-cm/9¾-inch square. Lay it in front of you on the diagonal, gently fold the top half down (to form an inverted triangle), then unfold it to form a light crease across the centre. Make a rough pile of ½ the nuts, just below this centre line. Spread ½ the chutney over one side of the cheese, and lay it chutney-side-down on the nuts, so the straight (cut) side of the cheese runs along the crease. Spread the remaining chutney on top and sprinkle over the remaining nuts.

3 Brush the exposed pastry lightly with egg wash and bring the top half of the pastry up and over the cheese, to enclose it completely. Use your hands to press the pastry into a snug fit all around and seal firmly. Trim away any excess pastry around the base with a knife or scissors, crimp firmly all around with the tines of a fork and trim again to neaten.

4 Transfer to a small baking tin or pan lined with baking parchment. Make a hole in the top, brush generously with egg wash and sprinkle with nigella seeds, if using.

5 Bake at 190°C fan/210°C/425°F for about 20–25 minutes, till golden and puffed. Leave for 5 tantalizing minutes before cutting in two and serving with salad. If your pastry springs a leak – it can happen even in Cornwall – spoon up any melted cheese and divide it between the plates.

TRICK OF THE TRADE

Toasted walnuts are well worth the extra trouble — more flavour,
more crunch. Spread them out on a baking tray or sheet and put
in the oven at 160°C fan/180°C/350°F for 8–10 minutes. If I buy
them in a pack, I toast the lot, and put those I don't immediately
need back in the pack for next time. My advice: toast walnuts till
they take on a glazed, bronzy appearance. And (learnt from bitter
experience) — always set a timer.

Cauliflower cheese & mustard soup with gruffins

This is simple comfort food. Put the unused cauliflower half in a bag in the fridge and use for tomorrow night's supper. I love cooking with Gruyère – fruity and nutty at the same time – but the recipe also works with Cheddar or blue cheese.

Gruffins (as we call Gruyère-topped muffins in our household) turn this into a tasty meal. If you swap the cheese, make chuffins or bluffins instead.

1 Wash the cauliflower half and discard the leaves. Use a small, thin knife to cut out the core, and slice the core lengthwise then into very thin pieces. Put in a medium saucepan (one with a lid). Slice right through the remaining cauliflower at 2-cm/¾-inch intervals and add the jumble of bits and florets to the pan.

2 Add the onion, stock, milk, butter, bay leaves and seasoning to the pan and bring to the boil (the cauliflower will be barely covered). Simmer, covered, stirring from time to time, until the cauliflower is soft, including the pieces of core – about 10 minutes.

3 Discard the bay leaves and stir in the mustard, nutmeg, cayenne and sherry. Transfer to a blender or small food processor (see Trick of the Trade) and whizz till as smooth as possible. Return to the pan and heat through: adjust the consistency with a little milk, if you wish. Add the cheese, check seasoning and heat through to melt, whisking. Try not to let it boil as this can turn the cheese stringy.

4 Meanwhile, preheat the grill/broiler to high and make the gruffins. Split the muffin (see Trick of the Trade) and lightly toast before spreading each cut side with a little butter and mustard. Top with the cheese and put under the hot grill till melting – 3–5 minutes. Slide onto waiting bowls of soup, add a grind of black pepper and serve with a spoon and fork.

½ small cauliflower
(about 375 g/13 oz.)
1 small onion, chopped
200 ml/6¾ fl oz./¾ cup stock,
cider (hard) or water
100 ml/3⅓ fl oz./⅓ cup plus
1 tbsp milk, plus a little extra
if necessary
25 g/2 tbsp butter
2 bay leaves
2 tsp Dijon mustard
a little freshly grated nutmeg
a pinch of cayenne pepper
3 tbsp dry sherry
50 g/1¾ oz./½ cup grated
Gruyère or mature/
sharp Cheddar

FOR THE GRUFFINS (OPTIONAL)
1 English muffin
a little butter
a little wholegrain mustard
35 g/1¼ oz./⅓ cup grated
Gruyère

TRICK OF THE TRADE

★ *One of my most trusted friends in the kitchen is my small food processor (see page 8). On rare occasions, I get out my **blender**. In general, this is not brilliant for small quantities – the blade at the bottom tends to miss them – but it is unbeatable when it comes to producing a super-smooth, velvety-textured soup. If you don't have a blender, process the soup thoroughly instead.*

★ *Although **English muffins** supposedly come from England, most British people miss out because they don't know a simple trick. Instead of slicing a muffin in half with a knife, work round the outside edge with the tines of a fork, pushing it in towards the centre. When you've been all the way round, lightly twist the muffin to separate. Result: a lovely textured surface which toasts to perfection, with lots of 'nooks and crannies' to hold the butter.*

Crunchy oven chicken

I hope this super-easy dish – which is reminiscent of Chicken Kiev, but less trouble and less butter – will become part of your weeknight repertoire, so I offer it in two versions. I am indebted to my friend Kristen Frederickson for the concept; in her delightful book of Anglo-American home cooking, Tonight at 7.30, she alleges that the recipe originally came from the back of a mayonnaise jar. It wouldn't surprise me – I have a lot of respect for 'commercial' recipe writers and on-pack instructions, though (bugbear alert!) I wish they were printed in larger type.

FOR THE CRUNCHY GARLIC CHICKEN

2 chicken breast fillets, skinless and boneless
4 tbsp grated Parmesan
5 tbsp mayonnaise
1 garlic clove, crushed
finely grated zest of ½ a lemon
2 tsp finely chopped fresh herbs (such as thyme, sage or rosemary)
50 g/1¾ oz. panko crumbs (about 5 small handfuls)
2 lemon wedges, to serve

FOR THE NUTTY CHICKEN

2 chicken breast fillets, skinless and boneless
4 tbsp grated Parmesan
5 tbsp mayonnaise
1 tsp Dijon mustard
½ tsp dried mixed herbs
20 g/¾ oz. nuts of your choice, finely chopped (by hand or in a food processor)
30 g/1 oz. panko crumbs (about 3 small handfuls)

The method is the same, whichever recipe you make.

1 Dry the chicken and discard the flaps and bits of fat. Stab through the thickest parts 5 times with a fork, season generously and set aside while you prepare your production line. Put the Parmesan, mayo, garlic, zest, herbs and seasoning (or Parmesan, mayo, mustard, herbs and seasoning) in a shallow dish and mix to a sticky paste using a spoon. Put the crumbs (or nuts and crumbs) and seasoning in a second dish, with a second spoon. Oil a rimmed baking tray or sheet or line with oiled foil or baking parchment, for easy clean-up.

2 Pick the first chicken fillet up by the tail and smear it all over with ½ the Parmesan mixture, using the spoon to make a thick covering. Now place it among the crumbs, using the second spoon to cover it completely on all sides. Lay on the baking tray and repeat. If you have crumbs left, sprinkle a few over the chicken. You can refrigerate this for 30 minutes if convenient.

3 Bake at 180°C fan/200°C/400°F for 25–30 minutes, till golden and cooked through. If you have a digital thermometer, it should read 65°C/149°F. Remove from the oven, cut into 3 or 4 thick slices and serve.

TRICK OF THE TRADE

Breaded chicken *is a favourite around the world. Flashed under a hot grill/broiler with tomato sauce and a slice of mozzarella on top, with spaghetti at the side, you have Chicken Parmesan. Or for a Japanese favourite, serve with rice and tonkatsu sauce. To make this BBQ-style sauce, which is also excellent with pork, mix 1 tablespoon tomato ketchup, 1 tablespoon Worcerstershire sauce, 1 teaspoon oyster or soy sauce, 1 teaspoon Dijon mustard, ½ teaspoon sugar.*

Caramel chicken with jasmine rice

This tasty dish is a celebration of Vietnamese flavours. If the idea of boiling sugar to make a caramel rings alarm bells, I urge you to venture forth and have a go. Some non-stick saucepans have a black interior which makes it harder to judge how dark the caramel has become, in which case turn all the lights on, and watch for the telltale wisps of smoke in step 3.

Bamboo shoots or water chestnuts add a pleasant crunch, but as you only need half a can and might waste the rest, you can skip them and serve mange-tout/snow peas on the side instead.

1 Trim the chicken thighs, discarding the flaps and bits of fat, and slice each crosswise into 3 or 4 pieces.

2 Take a medium saucepan, large enough to hold the chicken pieces in a single layer, and sprinkle the sugar over the base, followed by 2 tablespoons of the water. Keep the remaining water standing by. Swirl the pan (but don't stir) over a medium heat to dissolve, then continue to boil over a high heat, swirling often, until the mixture turns pale gold (3–5 minutes).

3 Turn the heat down to medium and continue to cook, watching like a hawk, until the mixture turns a mahogany colour and emits the odd (dragon-like) puff of smoke – 2–5 minutes longer. Remove from the heat and with great care pour in the remaining water – it will hiss and bubble like fury. Stir the lumpy mess over a medium heat until the caramel dissolves.

4 Stir in the fish sauce, garlic and bamboo shoots, if using, then the chicken. Simmer gently for about 25 minutes, stirring occasionally, until the chicken is tender. Dissolve the cornflour in 2 teaspoons of cold water and whisk into the sauce, simmer till it thickens slightly. (Fish sauce is salty, so you won't need seasoning.) Serve topped with shredded spring onions, if liked, and jasmine rice on the side.

3 or 4 chicken thighs, boneless and skinless (400–500 g/ 14–18 oz. total weight)
4 tbsp caster/superfine sugar
150 ml/5 fl oz./²⁄₃ cup water
2 tbsp fish sauce or soy sauce
2 garlic cloves, sliced
½ a 225-g/8-oz. can bamboo shoots or sliced water chestnuts, drained (optional)
2 tsp cornflour/cornstarch
2 spring onions/scallions, shedded, to garnish (optional)
jasmine rice, to serve (see Trick of the Trade)

TRICK OF THE TRADE

The sauce is so tasty I like to serve it with lots of jasmine rice, which I cook by the **absorption method.** *Put 130 g/4¾ oz./½ cup of jasmine rice in a pan with salt and pour over 225 ml/scant 1 cup boiling water (the ratio is 1 part rice to 2 parts water). Bring to the boil, then put on the lid and simmer on a very low heat for 15–20 minutes, until all the water has been absorbed and the rice is tender. Fluff with a fork and serve, or keep warm in the pan till ready.*

Easy cheesy enchiladas

Mexican food is one of the great cuisines of the world, stretching back to 7000BC – subtle, vibrant and inventive. My discovery of it has been via Tex-Mex and its tasty burritos (which were actually invented in the San Francisco Mission district), enchiladas, fajitas, nachos, quesadillas and tacos – all of which involve tortillas in one form or another. My friend Marlena Spieler – an expert in these cuisines – tells me that although tortilla is a Spanish word, the Aztecs and Incas were eating flat, corn-based cakes long before flour arrived with the Spanish.

'Whenever I want to feel happy,' says Marlena, 'I think about the wonderful enchiladas of New Mexico, which are made like cakes, and topped with a fried egg. You can order them in red sauce, or green sauce, and if you want both (I always do) you order: Christmas.'

This recipe is an easy introduction to an appealing, adaptable cooking style. If you don't have a fresh chilli/chile or a convenient jar of jalapeños in the the fridge, just miss them out. Mexican bottled sauces are an excellent standby – Marlena's favourite is Cholula. You can switch the cheese according to what you have available – here the feta is standing in for the Mexican Cotija, a hard, crumbly cows' milk cheese, but if you can get Cotija where you are, do use that.

For some reason, small tortillas are usually sold in packs of ten. Twelve I could understand – six would be helpful – but ten? Anyway, extras can be frozen for another time.

1 onion, preferably red
1 (bell) pepper, red or green, deseeded
1 tbsp oil
1–3 tsp chilli/chili powder
1 tsp dried oregano
1 tbsp flour
2 garlic cloves, crushed
1 small fresh chilli/chile, deseeded and thinly sliced
230-g/8-oz. can chopped tomatoes, or ½ a 400-g/14-oz. can
100 ml/3⅓ fl oz./⅓ cup plus 1 tbsp stock, or water
a pinch of sugar
6 small flour tortillas
150 g/5½ oz./1½ cups grated Cheddar
75 g/2¾ oz./½ cup crumbled feta
3 tbsp soured cream, plus extra to serve
chopped fresh coriander/cilantro, to garnish (optional)

1 Slice the onion and pepper, then heat the oil in a large frying pan and fry quite gently for 12–15 minutes, till nicely browned. Stir in the chilli powder (to taste), oregano, flour, garlic and fresh chilli and fry for a minute, then gradually mix in the tomatoes, stock, sugar and seasoning. Simmer gently for 5 minutes, till thickened.

2 Lay the tortillas out on your work surface. (If they seem too stiff to roll, warm in a pan, the oven or microwave till pliable.) Distribute ¾ of the grated Cheddar between the tortillas, placing it in a line across the centre, and top with all the feta and 3 tablespoons of soured cream.

3 If your pan is ovenproof and you wish to bake these in the pan, arrange the tortillas seam-side down in the pan and spoon over the sauce to cover. Otherwise, sloop a little sauce over the base of an ovenproof dish, arrange the tortillas on top and spoon over the remaining sauce, trying to cover the tortillas completely. Either way, sprinkle with the remaining grated Cheddar and bake at 190°C fan/210°C/425°F, covered with foil, for 15 minutes, then remove the foil and bake for 5 minutes longer. Allow to cool for a few minutes before adding a sprinkling of chopped coriander, if you like, and serving with the extra soured cream.

Devilled pork steaks

Pork steaks slow-roasted under a crunchy mustard and cornflake crust are especially tender and tasty. This method was pioneered by the ingenious test chefs at Cooks' Illustrated, and yes, that oven temperature is correct. I like to serve these with a squeeze of lemon and – for a retro touch – cauliflower cheese and any green vegetable in season.

If you baulk at buying a lifetime supply of cornflakes (why are the boxes so enormous?), you can use panko crumbs instead – brown them in a little butter first – or pretzels, whizzed to crumbs in a food processor.

If you use loin pork chops and they arrive with the fat intact – don't waste it. See Trick of the Trade to learn how to convert it into super-crunchy crackling for now or another occasion.

1 Wipe the pork steaks dry with a piece of kitchen paper towel. Brush or wipe one side of each with a little oil (to prevent sticking) and lay oil-side down on a rack on a small rimmed baking tray or sheet. Mix the garlic, mustards, sugar and Tabasco with plenty of salt and pepper in one small bowl. Mix the cornflakes, paprika and chilli flakes in another.

2 Brush or smear the sides and tops with the mustard mixture (I use a small rubber spatula), then spoon the cornflake mixture on top and press on lightly. Don't worry too much about the sides.

3 Roast the steaks at 120°C fan/140°C/280°F for 40–45 minutes, till tender when poked with a knife and the meat is cooked. If you have a digital thermometer, the meat should read about 60°C/140°F. Allow to rest for 5–10 minutes before serving, with lemon wedges, if you like.

TRICK OF THE TRADE

*Pork loin chops sometimes arrive with a thick rubbery band of fat and skin running down one side. Sharpen your knife before cutting this away. This strip of fat and skin, ideally about 1 cm/¾ inch thick, makes marvellous **pork crackling**. I put the strips in the freezer till I need them – you can roast them from frozen.*

Put a piece of baking parchment in a smallish rimmed baking tin or pan, then lay on the well seasoned strips. Lay another piece of parchment on top, then another smaller baking tin on that, so the pork strips are weighed down and lying flat. Bake at 180°C fan/200°C/400°F for 50 minutes, turning the strips at half time. Serve sprinkled with plenty of flaky salt and (chef's tip) a light sprinkling of sugar.

If you are a crackling aficionado, I would also urge you to visit pages 110 and 141 You are in for a treat.

2 pork steaks or chops
  (150–175 g/5½–6 oz. each)
a little oil
1 small garlic clove, crushed
1 tbsp each Dijon and
  wholegrain mustard
½ tsp dry mustard powder
½ tsp sugar
a splash of Tabasco
about 20 g/¾ oz. cornflakes
  (2 handfuls), crushed by
  squeezing in your hand
½ tsp paprika or smoked
  paprika
a pinch of crushed chilli/hot red
  pepper flakes
lemon wedges, to serve
  (optional)

Fish fillets with a dill crust

This is an adaptable dish, which works for any fish fillets. Because fillets vary in thickness, a good guide is to allow 4 minutes of baking time per 1 cm/⅜ inch of thickness.

You can also vary the topping, according to what snacks or savoury biscuits/crackers you have lying around – just be sure to make sure they are well crushed in step 1.

FOR THE TOPPING

15 g/½ oz. cheese biscuits/
    crackers, crisps, pretzels,
    or other snacks, broken into
    small pieces (1 small handful)
3 tbsp panko crumbs
15 g/1 tbsp butter
a small handful of fresh dill,
    finely chopped
1 tsp creamed horseradish
2 tsp mayonnaise

FOR THE FISH

2 fish fillets, such as salmon,
    cod or haddock, with or
    without skin (about 120 g/
    4¼ oz. each)
a splash of olive oil
2 lemon wedges

1 Pulse the cheese biscuits in a small food processor to rough crumbs, add the panko crumbs and pulse again. Melt the butter in a small pan and fry the crumb mixture for 3–4 minutes, till fragrant, golden and lightly toasted. Take off the heat and stir in the dill.

2 Dry the fish, brush all over with oil and season generously with salt and pepper. Place the fish – if it has skin, skin-side down – on a small rimmed baking tin or pan, lined with foil. Mix the horseradish and mayonnaise and spread evenly on top of the fish, then sprinkle over the crumbs and press on gently. You can refrigerate at this point for up to an hour.

3 Add the lemon wedges to the baking tin and bake at 160°C fan/180°C/350°F for 13–18 minutes (depending on thickness), checking the centre is translucent when poked with a knife. If you have a digital thermometer, it should read 52°C/126°F. To serve, slide a spatula under each fillet (if the skin sticks to the foil, so much the better), and serve with a hot lemon wedge.

TRICK OF THE TRADE

*For those of us unable to grow fresh herbs in the garden, bought herbs are often unsatisfactory – the main problem being that the packs are too big, and you end up throwing half away. **Fresh dill** is a good example – there is no substitute for it, but you only want it occasionally, in moderate quantities.*

Over the years, I've worked out how to store most herbs so they last a bit longer (see page 108), but dill requires special treatment. One option is to freeze it. Wash and dry the dill thoroughly and freeze it in a small plastic box, to keep the fronds intact. Chop finely, still frozen, and separate any clumps. You can also dry dill, by tying small bunches with a piece of string and hanging from a cupboard knob, before crumbling the dried fronds and putting them in a screwtop jar. Enjoy little wafts of dill scent as the bunches dry.

Chicken Alsace

This recipe was the signature dish of my partner's grandmother, Marie-Antoinette, who emigrated to the United States from Strasbourg in 1925. (Being born in the 'swing region' of Alsace-Lorraine to determinedly French parents, she was christened the most French name they could think of.) It is practically effortless and – perhaps surprising, considering its vintage – healthy, too.

In northern France, butter is the usual cooking medium (as opposed to olive oil in the south), but Marie-Antoinette, ahead of her time in many ways, always used corn oil. I stir in a few scraps of butter at the end, to gloss up the sauce, but see what you think. You can use any white wine, though in honour of the recipe's origin, the best choice is a dry Riesling from Alsace.

Paprika is a very mild spice – don't hold back. For some reason, that tasty spice mix 'Old Bay Seasoning' has never caught on in the UK. If you are lucky enough to procure some, add a good sprinkle at the same time as the paprika.

Serve this with boiled long grain rice (add a little pot or cube of stock to the cooking water), and, if you wish, broccoli. Plus – needless to say – a glass of the vin d'Alsace, well chilled.

1 Trim the chicken breasts, discarding the flaps and bits of fat. Sprinkle a plate generously with flour and paprika and roll the chicken around to cover completely.

2 Heat the oil in a large frying pan or skillet (one with a lid) and fry the chicken for 3–4 minutes per side, till nicely browned. Transfer to a plate. Add a little extra oil to the pan if necessary and fry the onion, celery and carrot for about 5 minutes, till softened, but not browned.

3 Use a spatula to form the vegetables into a low mound in the centre of the pan. Lay the chicken breasts on top and season well with salt, plenty of pepper and a really good sprinkling of paprika. Pour the wine around the outside of the pan and bring to a good simmer. Cover and simmer for about 7 minutes, then flip the chicken, season as before, and cook, covered, for another 7 minutes. 2–3 minutes before the end, lift off the lid and, if you would like to reduce the sauce, finish the cooking uncovered. The vegetables should retain some texture. Check for seasoning, adding a good pinch of salt to moderate the flavour if you feel it is too winey, and bits of butter, if you wish.

4 To serve, lay each chicken breast on a bed of rice, surround with the vegetables and pour the sauce over it all. Add a sprinkle of chopped parsley, if liked, and serve.

2 chicken breast fillets, skinless and boneless
a little flour and a few pinches of paprika
1 tbsp oil, or corn oil, plus a little extra if necessary
1 onion, roughly chopped so it retains some texture
2 sticks/stalks celery, thinly sliced
1 large carrot, grated on the large holes of a box grater
200 ml/6¾ fl oz./¾ cup dry Riesling wine, or a mixture of wine and chicken stock
15 g/1 tbsp butter, to finish (optional)
a little chopped fresh parsley, to garnish (optional)

Lemon & coconut soup with flatbreads

This flavoursome Thai-inspired soup is accompanied by simple flatbreads, and although simple to make, relies on authentic ingredients.

I don't often encounter fresh galangal (its spot in the grocery section seems to have been supplanted by fresh turmeric) so I buy it when I see it. Like fresh ginger, it can be stored in the freezer and used from frozen. Lime leaves – properly called makrut lime leaves (not 'kaffir', which is offensive) – are available dried or fresh, and give an essential zing.

FOR THE FLATBREADS

100 g/3½ oz./¾ cup minus
   ½ tbsp strong white/bread
   flour, plus extra for dusting
50 g/¾ oz./heaping ⅓ cup
   wholemeal/whole-wheat flour
1 tsp sugar
¾ tsp salt
110 ml/3⅓ fl oz./½ cup minus
   2 tsp hand-hot water
½ tsp instant dried yeast
25 g/2 tbsp butter, melted

FOR THE SOUP

a 3-cm/1¼-in. piece each of
   fresh ginger and galangal
   (if you can find it)
2 lemongrass stems
6 lime leaves, dried or fresh
200 ml/6¾ fl oz./¾ cup chicken
   stock
½ a 400-ml/14-fl oz. can
   coconut milk
1 chicken breast fillet,
   skinless and boneless
2 firm mushrooms, sliced
75 g/2¾ oz./1 cup cooked and
   peeled prawns/shrimp

TO SERVE

2 spring onions/scallions,
   shredded
juice of ½ a lime
1 tbsp fish sauce
a small handful of chopped
   fresh coriander/cilantro
1 small red chilli/chile,
   deseeded and thinly sliced

1 To make the flatbreads, mix the first 6 ingredients in a bowl to make a soft, sticky dough. Cover and leave to rise somewhere warm for 1½ hours, then roll out on a well floured surface into a 20-cm/8-inch square about 1 cm/⅜ inch thick. Brush lightly with a little of the melted butter and roll up into a tight sausage. Cut into 4 fat discs, stand them upright and squash each one down with the palm of your hand. Dust with flour, put on a plate and refrigerate until ready to cook.

2 To make the soup base, finely chop the ginger and thinly slice the galangal. Trim and bruise the lemongrass, before cutting it into 5-cm/2-inch lengths. Put these in a pan and add the stock and coconut milk. Simmer, covered, for 15 minutes, then set aside for up to 1 hour to infuse.

3 Strain the soup base and return it to the pan. Cut the chicken into bite-size pieces and stir it in. Add the mushrooms and simmer for 5–7 minutes, till the chicken is cooked, then stir in the prawns. Keep warm until ready to serve.

4 To cook the flatbreads, heat a large dry frying pan (no oil) till hot. Roll the pieces of dough into 13-cm/5-inch ovals (so two can fit in the pan, side by side), about 1 cm/⅜ inch thick. Brush the tops with ½ the remaining butter, then place the first two in the pan, butter-side down. While they cook, brush the tops with more melted butter, then once they start to puff – about 2 minutes – flip and cook the other side for 2 minutes. Keep warm while you cook the two remaining flatbreads.

5 Stir the spring onions, lime juice, fish sauce and chopped coriander into the soup and warm through, pour into bowls, sprinkle with chilli slices and serve with the flatbreads.

TRICK OF THE TRADE

Fresh coriander/cilantro is one herb which you can roughly chop in its entirety – stems and all – so don't waste time picking off the leaves, unless you really feel you must.

Pork & aubergine stir-fry

I like to take a methodical approach to stir-fries, preparing everything and lining it up before I start. For the person you are cooking for, this can be alarming (why is nothing happening?), but the result is fresh and full of impact. Serve this feisty dish, packed with Chinese flavour, with plain white rice.

If you can only buy a large aubergine/eggplant, you will find a recipe for Ratatouille Cannelloni on page 112, which will make good use of the remaining half.

1 Mix the rice wine, soy, sesame oil, sugar and vinegar in a small bowl. Slice the pork fillet down the centre, then into very thin slices. Put in a second bowl, sprinkle with the cornflour and, using a spatula, stir in 1 tablespoon of the wine mixture until the pork is sticky all over.

2 Put the aubergine and onion in a large bowl. Peel and finely chop the ginger, slice the garlic and put in a small bowl with the chilli flakes.

3 Now get cooking. Heat 1 tablespoon of oil in a large frying pan or wok and add the aubergine and onion. Season and – keeping the heat high – sizzle for 8–10 minutes, adding a splash more oil if it looks dry, till tender and beginning to take on colour, then return to the bowl. Next into the hot pan goes a splash more oil and the pork. Cook, stirring energetically, for 3–4 minutes, till just cooked. Remove to the bowl with the aubergine. Finally, put the ginger mixture in the pan and sizzle for 1 minute, then return the aubergine and pork to the pan and pour over the remaining wine mixture. Stir to heat through and serve garnished with scattered basil leaves, if using (or make a chiffonade, see below).

TRICK OF THE TRADE

Recipes often advise to 'tear' basil rather than chop it, and this seems the right approach for dishes where an assertive bite of basil breaks up the potential monotony of a dish – for instance pizza. Chopping doesn't really work – the basil taste seems to disappear – but a useful alternative is slicing, or technically, making a **chiffonade***. It's a satisfying little operation. Pick out the biggest leaf of basil from a bunch and lay it flat on the board. Now pick out more leaves and stack them flat on top. Keeping it as tidy as you can, roll the stack up from the longer side, to make a tight sausage. (At this stage, I usually put a wire twist around the base, and put it in the fridge till I need it.) When the moment comes, take the twist off, hold the sausage on the board using one hand and slice as finely as you can with the other, to make super-thin strips. This technique is also used to make the seaweed on page 123.*

3 tbsp Shaoxing rice wine
  or dry sherry
3 tbsp soy sauce
a splash of toasted sesame oil
2 tsp sugar
1 tsp Chinese vinegar or white
  wine vinegar
1 small pork fillet (about 425 g/
  15 oz.), trimmed
1 tsp cornflour/cornstarch
1 small aubergine/eggplant
  (200–250 g/7–9 oz.), or ½
  a large one, not peeled, cut
  in 2–3-cm/¾–1¼-in. cubes
1 small onion, sliced
a 3-cm/1¼-in. piece of fresh
  ginger
5 garlic cloves
½ tsp crushed chilli/hot red
  pepper flakes
2–3 tbsp oil
fresh Thai basil or basil,
  to garnish (optional)
  (see Trick of the Trade)

Simple nasi goreng

There are perhaps as many variations on this fabulous Indonesian egg-and-rice dish as there are islands in Indonesia (at the last count, 17,508). It is tasty and satisfying, the more so if you invest in authentic ingredients: kecap manis (Indonesian sweet soy sauce) and terasi (Indonesian shrimp paste – Thai shrimp paste is similar). I have suggested more mainstream ingredients in case you can't find the real thing.

Traditionally this dish is built around leftover cooked rice. If you do this, make sure the rice was properly cooled and that you heat it through thoroughly here. The texture will be less authentic, but you can also use freshly cooked rice. (I would happily recommend the microwaveable packs – the plain versions are perfectly acceptable – except you will likely be left with half a pack over.)

This is essentially street food, and the fun part is to pile the spicy rice with toppings. My favourite is a fried egg – which seems to bring the whole dish together – but take your pick, or experiment with leftovers. By all means make this meat-free, but if using cooked meat or fish, these can be added and heated through in step 3. This is an easy dish to make, but you will need seven or eight small bowls in which to marshal your ingredients before you start cooking.

140 g/5 oz./¾ cup long-grain rice, or about 425 g/15 oz./3½ cups cooked rice (see recipe introduction)
2 shallots, sliced
1 or 2 garlic cloves, roughly chopped
1 fresh green chilli/chile, thinly sliced
1 tbsp terasi (Indonesian shrimp paste), or tomato purée/paste
1 tbsp water
2–3 tbsp oil
1 tbsp kecap manis (Indonesian sweet soy sauce), or use 1 tbsp soy sauce plus 1 tsp sugar
1 tsp fish sauce (optional)
1 egg, any size, beaten with salt and pepper
a handful of frozen peas (no need to defrost)

about 75 g/2¾ oz./ generous ½ cup slivered ham (optional)
about 75 g/2¾ oz./1 cup cooked and peeled prawns/shrimp (optional)

FOR THE TOPPINGS
any or all of the following:
2 spring onions/ scallions, sliced on the bias
2 fried eggs
¼ cucumber, sliced and seasoned
1 tomato, quartered and seasoned
a sprinkle of chopped dry-roasted peanuts

TO SERVE
prawn/shrimp crackers (optional)

1 If cooking the rice from scratch, follow your preferred method. Whizz 1 shallot, the garlic, chilli, terasi, water and 1 tablespoon oil in a small food processor to make a paste. This is a small quantity even for a small processor, so wipe down the bowl as necessary, or use a pestle and mortar. In a small bowl, mix the kecap manis and fish sauce (if using).

2 Heat the remaining oil in a medium frying pan, add the remaining shallot, season and fry till brown, 3–4 minutes. Transfer to a small dish. Add a splash more oil if necessary and pour in the beaten egg, stirring around for about 30 seconds to make a mini-omelette (it doesn't have to be very tidy). Slide this onto a board and roll into a tight sausage. Add the shallot paste to the pan and fry until golden, about 3 minutes.

3 Add the rice to the pan, pour over the kecap manis and stir everything together till hot. Slice the omelette into thin strips and stir in, along with the fried shallot, plus the ham and prawns, if using. Season to taste and heat through.

4 Mound in bowls and top with spring onion and any other toppings. Serve with prawn crackers, if you like.

Paella in the oven

Paella is one of Spain's most important contributions to the culinary world, and I feel privileged many years ago to have savoured the real thing, cooked in a huge pan before me, under the shade of an orange tree, and washed down with a glass of chilled white Rioja. There are many incarnations of this noble dish for both cook and gourmet to explore, and I offer this simplified, streamlined version in a spirit of humility – and because I love paella.

This is best served piping hot from the pan, just as it is, or with crusty bread and a salad.

1 Preheat the oven to 200°C fan/220°C/450°F. Put the stock, chopped tomatoes, paprika, bay leaf and saffron in a large, heatproof jug/pitcher or bowl and microwave on high for about 5 minutes, until steaming hot.

2 Put the cherry tomatoes, onion and garlic in a roomy, flameproof roasting tin or pan, drizzle over the oil and mix to coat. Cook in the oven for 15 minutes, until beginning to brown.

3 Stir in the rice, chicken, chorizo, rosemary and hot stock mixture. Bring to the boil on the hob/stovetop, season well, then return to the oven for 20 minutes (don't cover).

4 Stir in the prawns, peas and sherry, lay the lemon wedges on top, and return to the oven for 5–10 minutes, until everything is cooked through and the lemon wedges are hot and juicy. Serve at once with the lemon wedges to squeeze over.

TRICK OF THE TRADE

Shopping for prawns/shrimp *is a confusing business. For everyday, the best approach is to buy large bags of frozen cooked ones (ASC or MSC means they have been sustainably fished). It feels like a bit of an investment, but you can simply lift out as many as you need at a time: defrost in water, changing the water every few minutes if you need to speed things up.*

300 ml/10 fl oz./1¼ cups stock
230-g/8-oz. can chopped
   tomatoes, or ½ a 400-g/
   14-oz. can
½ tsp smoked paprika
1 bay leaf
a good pinch of saffron threads
10 cherry tomatoes
1 small onion, chopped
1 garlic clove, crushed
1 tbsp olive oil
125 g/4½ oz./⅔ cup paella rice
2 chicken thigh fillets, skinless
   and boneless, halved
35 g/1¼ oz. cured chorizo, cut
   into thin semi-circles (see
   Trick of the Trade, page 71)
a small handful of fresh
   rosemary leaves, chopped
75 g/2¾ oz./1 cup cooked
   prawns/shrimp, unpeeled
   (see Trick of the Trade)
a handful of frozen peas
   (no need to defrost)
50 ml/1⅔ fl oz. dry sherry
   (about ½ a glass)
2 lemon wedges

Stuffed vegetables in the Greek style

*This all-in-one supper, which was inspired by a recipe in Tessa Kiros's Falling Cloudberries,
will bring a taste of sunshine to your table, whatever the weather.*

*You can use any minced/ground meat for this – even a couple of sausages, skins removed,
will do. You can cook this in an ovenproof dish rather than a tin but if so, bring the stock to the boil
before adding it at the end of step 3. To serve, slice the vegetables in two, so you both get to enjoy all
the flavours. I like the surprising crunch of a coriander seed, but if you don't, simply omit them.*

25 g/1 oz./¼ cup long grain
    or risotto rice
1 medium courgette/zucchini
2 medium, firm tomatoes
1 yellow (bell) pepper
2–3 potatoes (depending on
    appetite), preferably red,
    unpeeled, cut into wedges
1 tbsp olive oil, plus extra for
    drizzling
1 red onion, chopped
150 g/5½ oz./¾ cup minced/
    ground lamb, beef or pork
1 garlic clove, crushed
½ tsp each ground coriander,
    cumin and cinnamon
a pinch of crushed chilli/hot red
    pepper flakes
50 g/¾ oz./⅓ cup crumbled
    feta
1 tbsp pine nuts
2 tbsp raisins, sultanas/golden
    raisins or currants
½ a lemon
a few sprigs of fresh mint and
    parsley
200 ml/6¾ fl oz./¾ cup stock,
    white wine, or a mixture
8 coriander seeds (optional)
pitted black olives and capers,
    to finish (optional)

1 Choose a pan large enough to hold the courgette and pepper, but first of all use it to cook the rice. Bring some salted water to the boil and cook the rice for 12–15 minutes till tender. Drain the rice over a jug/pitcher and transfer to a large bowl. Return the cooking water to the pan. Meanwhile, prepare the vegetables. Trim the courgette, take a long slice off the top and use a spoon to hollow the flesh out – taking care to get the ends as thin as the sides. It should look a bit like a canoe. Chop the innards of the courgette finely and put in a small bowl. Slice a hat off each of the tomatoes and scoop out the inside. Chop the innards and add to the bowl. Slice the pepper lengthwise through the stem, this time discarding the innards. Put the prepared courgette and pepper in the pan and add the potatoes, and add more boiling water if necessary, to cover. After 3 minutes, remove the pepper, then the courgette. Continue cooking the potatoes for 7–9 minutes, till just tender, then drain.

2 Heat the oil in a medium frying pan and fry the onion for 5 minutes, until starting to brown. Add the meat and fry till no longer pink, about 4 minutes, breaking it up as it cooks. Add the garlic and spices and cook for 1 minute. Stir into the cooked rice, along with the feta, pine nuts, raisins, zest of the ½ a lemon and ½ of the fresh herbs, chopped. Taste and season generously. Divide the stuffing between the vegetables and top the tomatoes with their hats. Put the chopped courgette and tomato innards from step 1 in a flameproof roasting tin or pan, then top with the stuffed vegetables and potatoes. Add the stock and bring to the boil on the hob/stovetop. Sprinkle a little salt on the potatoes, scatter over the coriander seeds, if using, and drizzle with extra olive oil.

3 Bake at 180°C fan/200°C/400°F for 35–40 minutes, turning the potatoes over halfway through, till the vegetables are soft. Five minutes before the end, add the lemon ½ into the tin to heat through. In Greece, this dish would be served warm or at room temperature, so if you can resist it, allow it to rest for 30 minutes. Squeeze over the lemon juice, sprinkle with the remaining herbs and, to add a touch more Mediterranean flair, black olives and capers, if you like.

Smoked mackerel kedgeree

There are many different ways to make kedgeree, but I like mine subtly spiced, and laced with strips of omelette rather than the usual hard-boiled egg. I enjoy the faintly medicinal crunch of cardamom pods in a dish, but if you don't, locate and remove them at the end of step 1. If you have a little smoked salmon or cooked and peeled prawns/shrimp to hand, these can be stirred in with the mackerel. For a more assertive curry flavour, add 1–2 teaspoons curry paste with the garlic.

In the days when I ran a restaurant, I used to luxe this dish up for Sunday brunch by serving a hollandaise alongside. Once you have eaten it with hollandaise, I promise there is no turning back. To make hollandaise, use my béarnaise method on page 120, substituting lemon juice for vinegar, and omitting the tarragon.

1 To cook the rice, heat the oil in a medium pan (one with a lid) and fry the onion for about 4 minutes, till golden. Add the garlic, bay leaf, cardamom, cinnamon, cumin and turmeric and sizzle for a minute, then add the rice and stir for a minute to coat with oil. Add the stock and salt, stir well and put on the lid. Turn the heat to the lowest possible simmer – check there is just the odd bubble breaking – and set the timer for 15 minutes. Do not stir. Turn off the heat and leave undisturbed for 10–15 further minutes.

2 Meanwhile, put the smoked mackerel fillets in a heatproof bowl and the frozen peas in another, and pour boiling water over each to submerge. Leave for 5–10 minutes. When ready, drain the fillets and use your fingers to peel away and discard the skin. Break into bite-size flakes and add to the pan of rice (still covered) along with the drained peas, to keep warm.

3 Heat the butter in a small frying pan till the foam has subsided. Beat the eggs with seasoning, the garam masala and a splash of water, then pour into the pan. Allow to set around the edges, then lift the edges with a spatula and allow the uncooked mixture to flow underneath. When cooked to a soft omelette, slide onto a board and use the spatula to cut into strips.

4 Now stir the rice mixture, omelette and parsley together. Taste for seasoning and heat briefly if necessary. Pile onto plates and serve with a knob/pat of butter on each serving and a lemon wedge at the side.

TRICK OF THE TRADE

*If you're 'lifting' a dish by serving a **wedge of citrus** alongside, the professional way to present it is to trim the point off each end of the fruit, then cut into sixths (oranges and lemons) or quarters (limes). Slice off and discard the seedy centre of each wedge and put each one, rind-side down, on a cutting board. Make a few cuts down into the flesh to stop the juice shooting into your eye when you squeeze it.*

FOR THE RICE
1 tsp oil
1 small onion, chopped
1 garlic clove, crushed
1 bay leaf
3 cardamom pods, crushed (optional)
½ tsp each ground cinnamon and ground cumin
a pinch of ground turmeric
90 g/3¼ oz./½ cup basmati rice (no need to rinse)
200 ml/6¾ fl oz./¾ cup boiling stock or boiling water
½ tsp flaky salt

FOR THE FISH
2 smoked mackerel fillets
100 g/3½ oz./¾ cup frozen peas (no need to defrost)

FOR THE SPICED OMELETTE
15 g/1 tbsp butter, plus extra for serving
2 eggs, any size
½ tsp garam masala (see Trick of the Trade, page 67)
a small handful of fresh parsley, chopped, to finish
lemon wedges, to serve (see Trick of the Trade)

Three-mushroom goulash

This tasty and substantial supper dish can be served with boiled potatoes (in the Hungarian style), rice or tagliatelle: if you have poppy seeds to hand, sprinkle on lightly to provide a soft crunch. Feel free to halve the quantity of tomatoes and add a small glass of red wine, if liked.

about 8 g/¼ oz. dried porcini mushrooms (see Trick of the Trade)

300 g/10½ oz./about 4 cups mixed fresh mushrooms

a splash of olive oil

15 g/1 tbsp butter

1 shallot, sliced

1 tbsp tomato purée/paste (see Trick of the Trade)

1 garlic clove, crushed

1 tsp smoked paprika, plus extra to garnish

½ tsp caraway seeds, lightly crushed in a spice mill or pestle and mortar

230-g/8 oz. can chopped tomatoes, or ½ a 400-g/ 14-oz. can

a splash of water, wine or stock, if necessary

a squeeze of lemon juice

200-g/7-oz. tub soured cream

a small handful of fresh parsley or tarragon, chopped

1 Put the porcini in a cup or heatproof bowl, cover with 100 ml/⅓ cup plus 1 tablespoon boiling water and set aside to steep while you trim the mushrooms. Slice any large mushrooms, halve or quarter smaller ones, but aim for a variety of shapes and sizes. Now line a small sieve/strainer with a piece of kitchen paper towel and place over a cup or jug/pitcher. Fish the porcini out of their soaking liquid (do not discard) with your fingers, rinse under the tap to remove any remaining grit and slice roughly. Pour the soaking juices into the sieve, allow the liquid to filter through and discard the kitchen paper towel and the bits caught in it.

2 Heat the oil and butter in a large frying pan and add the shallot. Cook over a medium heat till starting to go brown – 2–3 minutes – then raise the heat and add the mushrooms and porcini. Some mushrooms release water, so just keep stirring and sizzling until any liquid has boiled away and the mushrooms are appealingly browned, about 5 minutes. Stir in the tomato purée, garlic, paprika and caraway and cook for 30 seconds.

3 Now stir in the porcini soaking juices and tomatoes and simmer till slightly thickened, about 5 minutes. Add a splash of water, wine or stock if necessary, to achieve a saucy consistency. Season well and add a squeeze of lemon juice to brighten the flavour.

4 When ready to serve, swirl in about ¾ of the soured cream and heat through. Check the seasoning and serve with the remaining soured cream and a sprinkle of paprika and chopped herbs.

TRICK OF THE TRADE

★ *I have never discovered why **porcini** should be contaminated with fine grit, but – as in the case of unwashed salad leaves – it's a horrible surprise to crunch on when you're not expecting it. After rehydrating in boiling water, I like to give the mushrooms a thorough rinse under the tap. You can throw the soaking juices away if you wish, but it is easy enough to filter them through a piece of kitchen paper towel, and they do contribute a little extra savouriness.*

★ ***Tomato purée/paste** adds depth of flavour but can taste slightly metallic. To avoid this, add it towards the end of frying and cook (or 'fry it off', in chef-speak) until you see it darken slightly. I always buy the type in a tube because it's so much more convenient than those tiny cans.*

STORECUPBOARD HEROES

A collection of ideas for suppers and lunches based around everyday ingredients, including some that can be easily swapped and customized according to what you have around. No leftovers – no half-used packs – everything serves two.

Antipasti tart

For lovers of Italian snacks and delicacies, this one is for you. You can adapt it according to what you have on hand, and it only takes 10 minutes to assemble.

For this recipe, I recommend using a ready-rolled puff pastry sheet. Unfortunately, these are sold in different shapes and sizes, but as a rough guide, you will need about 150–180 g/5½–6¼ oz. of pastry – approximately half a sheet. If you can only find block pastry, which most often comes in 500-g/18-oz. blocks, cut in half and freeze the unused half for another time: roll out the rest to the thickness of a pound coin (be prepared for some wastage). The other half, once defrosted, can be rolled out and used for Cheese Baked in Puff Pastry on page 16.

150–180 g/5½–6¼-oz. ready-rolled puff pastry (½ a pack)

1 tbsp pesto (see Trick of the Trade)

1 large tomato, sliced (about 50 g/1¾ oz.)

about ½ a 150-g/5½-oz. tub of prepared antipasti vegetables of your choice (artichokes, mushrooms, roasted peppers)

2 anchovy fillets, roughly chopped (optional)

about 75 g/2¾ oz. firm mozzarella, roughly crumbled, or other cheese of your choice

a handful of pitted black olives, or mixed olives, halved (optional)

fresh basil leaves, to finish (optional)

1 If necessary, lightly roll the pastry on a sheet of baking parchment to a rectangle about 23 x 17 cm/9 x 6¾ inches. Run a knife around lightly, about 1.5 cm/⅝ inch in from the edge, which will provide a crust. Prick the centre section all over with a fork.

2 Spread the centre section evenly with the pesto, arrange the tomato slices and assorted antipasti on top, then dot with bits of anchovy, if using, cheese and olives. Season with a good grinding of black pepper.

3 Bake at 180°C fan/200°C/400°F for about 15 minutes, turning at half time. Grind over a little extra pepper, strew with basil leaves, cut into portions and serve.

TRICK OF THE TRADE

*The clever people of Liguria, the birthplace of **pesto**, have let their imaginations run riot, and now produce pestos in every shade of the rainbow. If you have a choice, go for the small jars or mini-pots, so that leftovers don't languish in the fridge making you feel guilty. You can use any pesto for this recipe.*

Fettuccine alfredissimo

Fettuccine Alfredo is the sumptuously rich signature dish of a famous restaurant in Rome's Via della Scrofa, dating back to 1907. I believe it is entirely in the right spirit to add strips of bacon and snipped chives to the dish, but lest my (even more OTT) version should be confused with the hallowed original, I have added issimo to the name.

The sauce adheres better to fresh pasta, but if you only have dried, use 165 g/6 oz. and add extra cooking water in step 4 to correct the consistency if necessary.

Unfortunately – or perhaps not – this is a dish that needs to be eaten immediately, and all in one go: the sauce splits if you try and reheat it. Have hot bowls ready for serving.

1 Melt the butter in a medium saucepan and fry the bacon in it till golden, 2–3 minutes. Remove the bacon to a small dish using a slotted spoon.

2 Add the cream to the pan and simmer for a minute, till slightly thickened. Mix the Parmesan and nutmeg in a bowl and add plenty of salt and a good grinding of black pepper.

3 Cook the pasta in a pan of well-salted water for the time indicated on the pack (typically 3–4 minutes). Fresh pasta has a tendency to boil over, so keep an eye on it. Scoop out a cupful of the cooking water, then drain the pasta, but not too thoroughly.

4 Add the pasta to the pan containing the cream, sprinkle over the cheese mixture and gently fold everything together over a medium heat, using a rubber spatula. Once the cheese is beginning to melt and stops looking granular, stir in 3 tablespoons of the reserved cooking water. It will at first look watery, but will thicken before your eyes. Add a splash more water if it is too thick. Check the seasoning, then serve in hot bowls, scattered with the chives and the bacon strips.

25 g/2 tbsp butter
2–3 rashers/slices of bacon, cut into strips
150 ml/5 fl oz./²⁄₃ cup double/ heavy cream
100 g/3½ oz./1½ cups finely grated Parmesan
a little freshly grated nutmeg
250 g/9 oz. fresh fettuccine or tagliatelle
a few fresh chives, snipped, to serve

TRICK OF THE TRADE

*I lived in Rome between the ages of 3 and 5, and according to my parents spoke Italian like a native. This is probably an exaggeration, but my mother did learn a thing or two about **cooking pasta**. One was that pasta should not be drained thoroughly – it should look wet in the colander. Don't shake it about too much. Also, always set aside a cupful of the cooking water before draining the pasta. This often comes in handy when you need to correct the consistency of a sauce, and has the advantage of being hot, ready-salted and slightly starchy. In this dish, as well as in spaghetti carbonara, the cooking water actually emulsifies with the other sauce ingredients, to form a glossy liaison.*

Italian meatloaf

Meatloaf is the epitome of comfort cooking, so it is a pity for couples and twosomes that most recipes are designed to feed a crowd, with humongous leftovers. If you don't want to be eating meatloaf for the rest of the week, these individual meatloaves are for you. Once you are happy with the basic formula, you can vary the flavourings. You can use a skinned sausage instead of minced/ground beef or pork. If you have access to fresh sage, use 6 leaves, chopped, instead of the oregano. If you have streaky bacon to hand, or even better, sliced pancetta, lay a slice or two on top of each meatloaf, after glazing and before the Parmesan.

In the States, the classic accompaniment is, of course, mashed potatoes. A baked potato with butter, or soured cream and chives, also does the trick.

FOR THE MEATLOAF

about 8 g/¼ oz. dried porcini mushrooms (1 small handful)
1 tbsp olive oil
1 small onion, or red onion, chopped
1 garlic clove, crushed
a generous squeeze of tomato purée/paste
½ tsp dried oregano
a pinch of crushed chilli/hot red pepper flakes
40 g/1½ oz./scant ½ cup grated firm mozzarella, or other cheese (optional)
2 tbsp grated Parmesan, plus 1 tbsp extra, to finish
3 tbsp panko crumbs
2 tbsp milk
1 egg yolk, any size
about 400 g/14 oz./2 cups minced/ground beef or pork

FOR THE GLAZE

2 tbsp tomato ketchup
1 tsp Dijon mustard
1 tsp balsamic vinegar or glaze

1 Put the porcini in a cup or heatproof bowl, cover with boiling water and set aside to steep. Heat ½ the oil in small ovenproof frying pan and cook the onion with seasoning till golden – about 5 minutes. Drain and rinse the porcini under running water, then chop finely. Add them to the onion pan along with the garlic, tomato purée, oregano and chilli flakes and cook for another minute. Set aside.

2 In a medium bowl, mix the mozzarella (if using), Parmesan, panko crumbs, milk, egg yolk and plenty of seasoning. Stir in the onion mixture, then use a spatula or your hands to mix in the meat lightly but thoroughly.

3 Heat the remaining oil in the pan (no need to wash the pan first). Take ½ the meat mixture and shape with your hands into a rough square, about 10 cm/4 inches square and 3–4 cm/1¼–1½ inches thick, and put in the pan. Repeat with the remaining meat mixture. Fry for 3–4 minutes, till the underside is nicely browned, then flip the meat, using a pair of spatulas (if it crumbles, just pat it back into shape) and brown the other side for 2 minutes.

4 Mix the glaze ingredients and brush over the top of each mini-meatloaf. Sprinkle with the extra Parmesan and bake at 160°C fan/180°C/350°F for 10 minutes, till brown and cooked through.

TRICK OF THE TRADE

*When browning meat, chefs often refer to the underside – the side which is cooked first – as the **presentation side**: for whatever reason, it usually does come out looking more golden and toothsome, thus looks better facing up.*

Mac & cheese soufflé

This is not one of those towering soufflés that collapses as you take it to the table – more a fluffed version of a family favourite. You can also add a little chopped ham or – trust me on this – tiny cubes of Spam.

For this recipe, I use a soufflé dish 16 cm/6¼ inches in diameter and 7 cm/2¾ inches high. I also have a straight-sided oval baking dish of the same capacity, measuring about 24 x 16 cm/ 9½ x 6¼ inches, and 5 cm/2 inches high, which serves just as well.

If I can get hold of fresh tomatoes grown in proper sunshine, I like to serve them as an uncomplicated salad alongside.

1 Grease your dish (see intro) with ¼ of the butter and sprinkle thickly with 2 tablespoons of the panko crumbs. Stand the dish on a small rimmed baking tray or sheet, to make it easier to move about.

2 Bring a pan of well-salted water to a rolling boil. Calculate the pasta cooking time by checking the timing on the pack (in micro-print) and adding ½ again. Put the pasta in the water, bring back to the boil, clap on the lid and turn off the heat. Set the timer. (After a couple of minutes, give the pasta a stir to stop it sticking together, then put the lid back on.) When the time is up, check the pasta is cooked, drain (not too thoroughly), then return to the pan. Stir in the Dijon and another ¼ of the butter to coat the pasta, then fold in the chives and Parmesan.

3 Meanwhile, make a white sauce. If using evaporated milk, make up to 200 ml/6¾ fl oz./¾ cup with milk or water. Put into a small saucepan with the remaining 25 g/2 tablespoons butter and flour and bring to a simmer, whisking constantly as it becomes thick and smooth – the whole operation takes less than 2 minutes. Transfer to a large bowl. Stir in the dry mustard, Tabasco, nutmeg and plenty of seasoning. Stir the egg yolks lightly into the sauce, followed by most of the cheese, then fold in the macaroni mixture.

4 Whisk the egg whites with a pinch of salt to soft peaks, then fold lightly into the macaroni mixture. Gently turn the mixture into the prepared dish and sprinkle with remaining cheese and panko crumbs. Bake at 160°C fan/180°C/350°F for 30–35 minutes, until firm, golden and crunchy on top. Serve sprinkled with Tabasco, if you wish. If you don't finish the soufflé all at once, put it back in the oven, ready for second helpings.

50 g/3½ tbsp butter
3 tbsp panko crumbs or fresh breadcrumbs
100 g/3½ oz./¾–1 cup dried macaroni
1 tsp Dijon mustard
a small handful of fresh chives, snipped
2 tbsp grated Parmesan
170-g/6-oz. can evaporated milk, or 200 ml/6¾ fl oz./¾ cup milk
25 g/1 scant oz./3 tbsp flour
½ tsp dry mustard powder
a splash of Tabasco, plus extra to serve
a little freshly grated nutmeg
2 eggs, any size, separated
100 g/3½ oz./1 cup grated Cheddar or Double Gloucester

Classic risotto with bacon & peas

Risotto is one of the best storecupboard stand-bys, enabling you essentially to make a gourmet dinner out of rice, stock, Parmesan and whatever comes to hand. I think of it as a 'Monday meal', made with fresh chicken stock after Sunday's roast. Here, I flavour the risotto with bacon and peas, but check your fridge for enticing scraps.

I usually grate my Parmesan in a food processor, but to finish a risotto, I risk my knuckles on a Microplane grater, which gives an attractive snowy effect.

400 ml/14 fl oz./1¾ cups chicken stock, preferably home-made (see Trick of the Trade, page 135)

a splash of olive oil

35 g/2½ tbsp butter

75 g/2¾ oz. bacon, chopped, or cubed pancetta or lardons

1 small onion, chopped

1 garlic clove, crushed

100 g/3½ oz./heaping ½ cup risotto rice

about 100 ml/3⅓ fl oz./⅓ cup (1 small glass) white wine or dry sherry

1 bay leaf

about 70 g/2½ oz./½ cup frozen peas (2 handfuls), (no need to defrost)

a small bunch of fresh parsley, chopped

4 tbsp grated Parmesan, plus extra to finish

1 Put the chicken stock in a pan and bring to the boil, then turn off the heat and cover to keep hot. Heat the oil and ½ the butter in a medium saucepan and add the bacon, onion and garlic. Cook gently for 5 minutes, till soft but not brown, then stir in the rice. Cook for 2–3 minutes until the rice is slightly translucent and starting to turn gold, then stir in the wine and bay leaf and bubble until the wine has been absorbed (1–2 minutes).

2 Set the timer for 18 minutes and add enough stock to cover the rice. Season. From now on, aim to keep the rice covered by a thin film of stock at all times, and at a gentle simmer. Stir frequently and add more stock as necessary. At 18 minutes, stir in the peas and bring back to the boil. At 19 minutes, check the rice is tender – it should still have a slight bite to it – and adjust the seasoning. Cook for another minute if necessary, then turn off the heat. Remove the bay leaf, if you wish, though if you leave it in, it will bring good fortune to the person to whom it is served.

3 Pause for a couple of minutes – time to lay the table. Then fold in the parsley, grated Parmesan and the remaining butter using a rubber spatula. Transfer to heated bowls, dust with extra Parmesan and serve.

TRICK OF THE TRADE

*Italian cooks know that after stirring a risotto for a solid 20 minutes, it is essential to leave it sitting undisturbed in the pan for 5 more before tucking in, 'so the ingredients get to know one another'. A generous pause between cooking and eating allows a **melding of flavours**, and I would recommend it for this recipe and all dishes with complex, layered flavours, such as the Cassoulet du Jour on page 96.*

Omelette aux œufs brouillés

Many years ago, I was enjoying breakfast in the Parisian sunshine, in one of those cafés in the Faubourg St-Germain, and someone on an adjacent table ordered œufs brouillés. What arrived didn't look like scrambled eggs at all – more like a gleaming omelette. All the time pretending to read my guidebook, I espied the customer dig in with his fork, and from the golden omelettey crust tumbled a fluffy mound of perfectly scrambled egg.

If you like omelettes and you like scrambled eggs, you'll enjoy this. I've described here how I make scrambled eggs, but by all means use your preferred formula and method. I like to add bacon, but mushrooms and cheese are other possibilities. Pile the scrambled egg onto the omelette as it finishes cooking, and then slide onto waiting plates.

1 Put ½ the butter in your favourite pan for scrambled eggs, and ½ in your omelette pan. Beat 2 eggs plus 1 yolk with the milk, cream and seasoning for the scrambled eggs. Beat the other 3 eggs plus 1 white with the water, Parmesan and seasoning for the omelette. (At this point, they look remarkably similar, so make a mental note which is which.)

2 Heat your scrambling pan and gently fry the bacon in the butter till it is beginning to colour – 1–2 minutes. Turn the heat down, add the egg and milk mixture and stir gently till starting to scramble.

3 Heat your omelette pan and observe the butter froth, then subside, then start to go brown and smell nutty. Now pour in the omelette mixture. As the omelette sets, lift up the edge and allow the uncooked egg to flow underneath. Repeat until there is no more flow of uncooked egg, and sprinkle with the cheese. Turn down the heat. With your other hand (it helps if you are an octopus), finish scrambling the eggs in the other pan.

4 When the omelette is set to your liking and the cheese is looking melty, tip the scrambled egg in a line on top. Fold the omelette over the scrambled egg, divide in 2 with a spatula and manoeuvre each half onto a hot plate. Finish with flaky salt, more freshly ground black pepper and the chives. In Paris, this would arrive with a small extra nut of butter melting on top, to add gloss and glamour.

25 g/2 tbsp butter
6 eggs, any size
1 tbsp milk
1 tbsp cream
1 tbsp water
1 tsp grated Parmesan
3 rashers/slices of bacon (I like smoked streaky), cut into strips
2 tbsp grated Gruyère or Cheddar
a pinch of flaky sea salt
a few fresh chives, snipped

TRICK OF THE TRADE

*I always serve hot food on **warmed plates**, but not so hot that the food sizzles when it touches them. In my lifetime, I have encountered people who insist on food being served as hot as possible (ideally scalding) but I aim for 'recently hot'.*

One-pan puttanesca

Pasta puttanesca may be something you feel you don't need a recipe for – tomato sauce with a few olives thrown in at the end. Done right and spiced up all'arrabbiata it's a super-tasty supper, cooked all in one pan – yes, including the spaghetti – and on the table in 30–40 minutes.

This includes quite a few polarizing ingredients – anchovies, olives and capers – but if you don't like them, simply miss them out. Raisins add a Sicilian flourish to this dish, but if they're not your thing, simply skip them. If you have 'nduja in the fridge, add 1 tablespoon along with the tomato purée/paste, to add a spicy richness.

For a meat-free version, omit the lardons and anchovies.

1 tbsp raisins, currants or sultanas/golden raisins (chopped if large)

1 tbsp capers, rinsed if salted

1 tbsp olive oil

1 onion, or red onion, sliced

60 g/2¼ oz./½ cup smoked lardons, chopped pancetta, or bacon pieces (optional)

3 anchovy fillets (optional)

3 garlic cloves

a generous squeeze of tomato purée/paste

1 tsp dried oregano

1–2 pinches of sugar (to taste)

½–1 tsp crushed chilli/hot red pepper flakes (to taste)

400-g/14-oz. can chopped tomatoes

400 ml/14 fl oz./1²/₃ cups water (I use the empty tomato can to measure, 1 canful)

150 g/5½ oz. dried spaghetti

3–4 tbsp Kalamata or other black olives, pitted and roughly chopped

grated Parmesan, to serve (see Trick of the Trade)

toasted pine nuts, to serve (optional)

a small handful of fresh parsley, finely chopped (optional)

1 Put the raisins and capers in a small bowl, cover with boiling water and set aside to soak. Heat the oil in a large frying pan (one with a lid) and add the onion and lardons, if using. Cook gently for a full 7–10 minutes, till golden and caramelized. Crush the anchovies and garlic – I put them both through my garlic crusher, anchovies first – and add to the pan with the tomato purée and oregano. Season to taste with the sugar, chilli flakes and salt and pepper and cook for 1–2 minutes.

2 Stir in the tomatoes, water and spaghetti (snapping it if necessary to fit in the pan) and bring to the boil. Cover the pan and simmer for the time suggested on the spaghetti packet – typically 8–12 minutes – stirring occasionally to ensure the pasta is immersed in the sauce. If towards the end of the time the mixture is looking wet, remove the lid to thicken slightly. Check the spaghetti is al dente – cooked by this method, it may need 2–3 minutes extra – then stir in the drained raisins and capers, plus the olives and parsley if using, to heat through. Check the seasoning – again, be generous – serve with lots of grated Parmesan and add a scattering of pine nuts and chopped parsley, if you wish.

TRICKS OF THE TRADE

★ *If you haven't encountered it, '**nduja** (pronounced en-doo-ya) is a spicy fermented salami paste from Calabria, the region which forms the toe of the Italian peninsula. Soft and spreadable, it can be mixed into savoury dishes whenever you fancy a bit of extra oomph – tomato sauces, on pizzas or even on toast.*

★ *Confession: I have almost entirely stopped **grating Parmesan** by hand since an Italian friend swore to me that her entire family – including Nonna – did it in the processor. For a special effect, such as on page 56, by all means risk your knuckles on a Microplane.*

Pasta with red pepper & walnut pesto

Jars of roasted red (bell) peppers are a great larder stand-by – if this recipe leaves you with half a jar, use it for the Red Pepper, Chorizo & New Potato Frittata on page 71.

This pesto is also great for livening up store-bought ravioli – a 250-g/9-oz. or 325-g/11½-oz. pack will be sufficient for two. I like to serve this with a crunchy green salad, topped with croûtons and finished with a lemony dressing.

1 Bring a pan of salted water to the boil for the pasta. First add the garlic clove and boil for 1 minute, then remove and reserve (see Trick of the Trade).

2 Cook the pasta to *al dente* using your preferred method (you might wish to use my method on page 55, and see Trick of the Trade, below).

3 Meanwhile, blitz the garlic, walnuts, herbs, chilli flakes, Parmesan and red peppers in a small food processor, or using a pestle and mortar. Add the oil, whizz to a rough paste and taste for seasoning.

4 Drain the cooked pasta and stir in the pesto, then serve topped with extra grated Parmesan.

1 garlic clove, roughly chopped (see Trick of the Trade)
200 g/7 oz. dried pasta, such as rigatoni or penne
25 g/1 oz./¼ cup walnuts, toasted (see Trick of the Trade, page 17)
a good handful of fresh parsley or basil, roughly chopped
a pinch of crushed chilli/hot red pepper flakes
2 tbsp grated Parmesan, plus extra to serve
80 g/3 oz. roasted red (bell) peppers (about ½ a 230-g/ 8-oz. jar, drained)
2 tbsp olive oil

TRICK OF THE TRADE

★ *To tame the harshness of **raw garlic**, boil it for a minute before crushing or chopping. To remove the smell from your chopping/cutting board, rub with raw, grated apple or potato. To remove the smell from your fingers, carefully rub them on the flat side of a stainless steel knife under a running tap.*

★ *Confession: I haven't boiled **dried pasta** for 20 years. The technique of immersing the pasta in a modicum of boiling water, then turning off the heat – which saves energy and means it will never boil over – was pioneered by none other than Elizabeth David. The pasta cooks in the just-boiled water, and continues to do so as the water cools. After a while, it stops cooking and merely stays hot. It's a win-win. Some cooks who follow this method leave the pasta in the water for the boiling time printed on the package (for al dente), but I prefer time-and-a-half, and spaghetti and larger shapes are fine for up to 20 minutes.*

Believe it or not, the same, very forgiving, technique works for fresh corn on the cob/ears of corn. Remove the husks and silks, immerse the cobs/ears in a big pan of boiling water, turn off the heat, cover and leave for anything between 10 and 30 minutes.

Tartiflette

You might be forgiven for thinking this is a traditional dish from the Alps, to be enjoyed in a mountain chalet, washed down with a glass of vin jaune to the jingle of distant cow bells. Prosaic as it might sound, this lovely supper dish was, in fact, invented by the Reblochon marketing department in the 1980s as a way to sell more cheese.

Reblochon de Savoie is certainly the best choice, and is now available all year round. If you can't find it, use another rich cows' milk cheese, such as Vacherin, Camembert or our wondrous British equivalent, Tunworth (see page 16). If the rind of your chosen cheese is tough, pare it off as thinly as you can; I generally leave it on.

If you don't have an ovenproof pan, transfer the mixture to a wide ovenproof dish at the end of step 3. If you wish to get ahead, you can make the dish to the end of step 3, then heat under the grill/broiler at the last minute.

Accompany this dish with a green or tomato salad, if liked.

2 medium potatoes (about 350 g/12 oz. total weight)

1 tbsp olive oil, plus a little extra if necessary

1 onion, sliced about 1-cm/³⁄8-in. thick

75 g/2¾ oz. smoked streaky bacon (about 2–3 rashers/slices), cut into 1-cm/³⁄8-in. strips

1 garlic clove, sliced

a pinch of crushed chilli/hot red pepper flakes

100 ml/3¹⁄3 fl oz./generous ¹⁄3 cup crème fraîche

125 g/4½ oz. Reblochon, or available alternative cheese

2–3 tbsp panko crumbs or fresh breadcrumbs

1 Peel and slice the potatoes about 1.5 cm/⁵⁄8 inch thick. Boil in salted water for 7–9 minutes, till just tender (see Trick of the Trade) and drain.

2 Heat the oil in a medium, preferably ovenproof, frying pan and fry the onion for about 7 minutes, till golden. Add the bacon and garlic and continue frying gently for a further 4–5 minutes, stirring occasionally, everything is golden. Remove the onion and bacon to a heatproof bowl, using a slotted spoon.

3 Set your grill/broiler to high. Add the potatoes to the pan and brown briefly – turn them frequently using tongs. There should be enough fat in the pan, but if not, add a splash more oil. This will take 3–4 minutes – it doesn't matter if they break up a bit. Return the onion and bacon to the pan, sprinkle with chilli flakes and seasoning and mix together lightly with the crème fraîche.

4 Cut the cheese into chunks and nestle among the potatoes. Scatter with panko crumbs and grill/broil for 5 minutes, till spotty brown.

TRICK OF THE TRADE

*Here is a foolproof test for checking if **boiled potatoes** are tender: poke one with a small, sharp knife, lift it out of the water, and if the potato slowly slides off the knife back into the water, it is done. This little trick works when boiling both old and new potatoes.*

Masala beans on toast

A fun and super-easy lunch or supper for fans of baked beans. It is also great piled onto, or tucked into, Indian breads and eaten by hand. The optional garam masala spice mix (see Trick of the Trade) is used for the recipe for Indian Butter Chicken with Palak Aloo on page 77.

1 Finely chop the shallot, chilli and garlic. Heat the oil in a medium saucepan (one with a lid) and fry the mixture for 1–2 minutes, till beginning to brown. Stir in the tomato purée and spices to form a thick paste and cook for 1 minute (enjoying the spicy smell), then add the tomatoes, beans, sugar and plenty of seasoning. Cover and simmer for 5 minutes, adding a splash of water if necessary.

2 Toast and butter the bread, taste the beans for seasoning (be generous) and pile onto the toast. If you wish, finish with a pinch of flaky salt and a sprinkling of garam masala.

TRICK OF THE TRADE

*I love making my own delicate and fragrant home-ground **garam masala**, but if you prefer ready-made, choose the best quality available: made properly, it contains precious ingredients, and they don't come cheap. But fresh, good-quality spices will make a real difference, so if necessary, make this an occasion to check and replenish your spice cupboard.*

The main business is extracting the cardamom seeds. Madhur Jaffrey suggests doing this in front of the television, but I find it requires full attention. I squash the pods by running over them firmly with a rolling pin, then pick out the seeds and put them in a bowl, discarding the papery pods. You can lightly blow over the bowl to remove any remaining chaff. Black cardamom seeds have a slightly smoky taste, the green ones taste fresh and floral.

2 tsp cardamom pods (about 20, producing about ⅔ teaspoon seeds)

3-cm/1¼-inch piece of cinnamon stick

½ tsp cumin seeds

½ tsp cloves (about 12)

½ tsp peppercorns

about ⅛ of a nutmeg, grated

Put all the ingredients in an electric spice grinder (or designated coffee grinder) and grind to a powder, then transfer to a small screwtop jar. This makes about 2 tablespoons and will keep for a month.

1 shallot
1 small fresh red chilli/chile
1 garlic clove
a splash of oil
a generous squeeze of tomato purée/paste
½ tsp each ground coriander, cumin and turmeric
230-g/8-oz. can chopped tomatoes, or ½ a 400-g/14-oz. can
400-g/14-oz. can cannellini beans, drained and rinsed
a pinch of sugar
2–4 slices of rustic white bread, plus butter for spreading
a pinch of flaky salt (optional)
a sprinkling of garam masala (see Trick of the Trade), to finish (optional)

Quick tomato soup & cheese toasties

I've devised this simple recipe so you don't need to get out scales or measuring spoons.
Canned tomatoes vary, so buy the best you can for this recipe, and Neapolitan
San Marzano ones if you get the chance.
To make the toasties, please note – you butter the outside of the sandwiches.
Despite having made this recipe many, many times, I still manage to get it wrong.

FOR THE SOUP
a generous knob/pat of butter,
    plus a little extra to serve
    (optional)
1 shallot, chopped
1 garlic clove, crushed
a generous squeeze of tomato
    purée/paste
400-g/14-oz. can plum
    or chopped tomatoes
400 ml/14 fl oz./1²⁄₃ cups stock
    or water (I use the empty
    tomato can to measure,
    1 canful)
a good pinch of dried oregano
a handful of fresh breadcrumbs
    or soft crusts, or ½ a slice of
    bread, roughly crumbled
2 tsp sugar, plus more if
    necessary
2 dollops of double/heavy
    or soured cream, to serve
    (optional)

FOR THE CHEESE TOASTIES
4 slices of bread
about 15 g/1 tbsp softened
    butter, for spreading
about 1 tbsp mayonnaise
2 thin slices of Cheddar,
    or other cheese
a handful of grated Gruyère,
    or other tasty cheese

1 Make the soup by heating the butter in a medium saucepan and frying the shallot and garlic for 2–3 minutes, till beginning to brown. Add the tomato purée and sizzle for a minute, then add the tomatoes, stock, oregano, breadcrumbs (which will act as a thickener), sugar and plenty of seasoning, and simmer for 4–5 minutes, stirring. Process in a blender (for a super-smooth soup) or a small food processor, or using a stick/immersion blender, then heat through. Check the seasoning (the sugar really brings the flavours together) and keep warm while you make the toasties.

2 Choose a frying pan large enough to hold 2 slices of bread side by side, and a saucepan lid that fits within the pan (to weigh down the toasties). Lightly spread one side of each slice of bread with the butter and mayonnaise, right to the edge. Lay the first 2 slices, butter-side down, in the pan, side by side. Place the cheese slices on the bread, then sprinkle thickly with the grated cheese. Top with the remaining bread slices, butter-side up. Lay a piece of baking parchment, or 2 suitable offcuts (I always seem to have scraps lying around), to cover the bread, then top with the saucepan lid, so that it weighs the sandwiches down. Turn on the heat and cook for 2–3 minutes, till the undersides are golden. Remove the lid and parchment, flip the sandwiches carefully – using a couple of spatulas – and cook for 2 more minutes, covered as before. When the bottom is toasted and the cheese melted, serve with the warm soup, into which you may wish to stir in a little extra butter and a swirl of cream.

Red pepper, chorizo & new potato frittata

A frittata (Italian) is started on the hob/stovetop and finished in the oven, whereas a tortilla (Spanish) is cooked entirely on the hob. In this flavoursome dish, I have tried to combine the best of both worlds.

1 Heat the oil in a medium frying pan (one with a lid) and fry the potatoes and seasoning, covered, for 20–25 minutes until golden and tender, shaking the pan occasionally. (If more convenient, you can do this in a small roasting tin or pan at 180°C fan/200°C/400°F for 25–30 minutes.) Add the chorizo for the last couple of minutes, then remove to a heatproof bowl with a slotted spoon (no need to wash the pan).

2 Mix the eggs, cream, flour, paprika, cheese and basil in a bowl with a good amount of seasoning.

3 Heat the butter in the same frying pan till the foam has died down, then pour in the egg mixture. After a minute, lift the edge (as if making an omelette) to let the uncooked egg flow underneath. When there is no more uncooked egg, scatter the potato mixture and red peppers over. Lower the heat and cook, covered, for 2–3 minutes, until you can look underneath and see (and smell) that the base has browned.

4 Scatter with a little extra cheese and bake, uncovered, at 170°C fan/190°C/375°F for 4–8 minutes, till golden and beginning to puff.

5 Remove from the oven, leave in the pan for a minute, then cut into slices with a spatula and slide onto plates to serve.

TRICK OF THE TRADE

Chorizo *is a confusing subject, including how to pronounce it. (Chor-ee-so or chor-ee-tho? Take your pick.) It comes in cured versions – like salami – which can be eaten as snacks; as fresh sausages (sometimes called 'cooking chorizo'), which need to be cooked; or even a paste. For this dish, use the cured variety, either picante (spicy) or dulce (mild), as you prefer.*

1 tbsp olive oil
150–200 g/5½–7 oz. baby new potatoes, scrubbed and halved
50 g/1¾ oz. cured chorizo, cut into thin semi-circles (see Trick of the Trade)
4 eggs, any size
4 tbsp double/heavy cream
2 tsp flour
1 tsp smoked paprika
75–100 g/2¾–3½ oz./¾–1 cup grated Cheddar, plus a little extra to finish
a small bunch of fresh basil, roughly chopped
20 g/1½ tbsp butter
80 g/3 oz. roasted red (bell) peppers (about ½ a 230-g/8-oz. jar, drained), sliced

FAKE-AWAY
FRIDAYS

If you like to start your weekend with a
home-made takeaway, you've come to the
right place. Mouthwatering versions of
all-time favourites, cleverly adapted for two.

Baja tacos with pico de gallo

If you feel like escaping to Mexico's Baja California for a sparkling evening on the Pacific waterfront, this is for you. Crunchy fish fillets are tucked into corn tortillas, then adorned with a selection of tasty toppings. It's the culinary version of a mariachi band, with its swaying guitars, violins and trumpets. Don't be put off because the recipe looks long – if you take it step by step, it falls nicely into place, and the only actual cooking is the fish. Before you do anything, finely grate the zest and squeeze the juice of a lime, which will be needed at various stages, and cut lime wedges to serve. Also set out a dish of crunchy tortilla chips and some guacamole in which to dip them, to add to the joy. (I find small tortillas more manageable and elegant than large ones, and if you enjoy online shopping, you can order 10-cm/4-inch ones, in which case allow 3 each.)

FOR THE PICO DE GALLO
(means literally
'rooster's beak')
1 medium tomato
2 spring onions/
  scallions, finely
  chopped
1 garlic clove, crushed
finely grated zest and
  juice of ¼ a lime
½ a fresh jalapeño or
  other small fresh
  chilli/chile, deseeded
  and thinly sliced
a small handful of fresh
  coriander/cilantro,
  chopped

**FOR THE PICKLED
RADISHES**
4 radishes, trimmed,
  halved and thinly
  sliced
juice of ½ a lime
½ a fresh jalapeño or
  other small chilli/
  chile, deseeded and
  thinly sliced
¼ tsp sugar
a good pinch of salt

FOR THE CREMA
½ a 150-ml/5 fl-oz. pot
  soured cream
4 tbsp mayonnaise
1 tbsp milk
finely grated zest and
  juice of ¼ a lime
a small handful of fresh
  coriander/cilantro,
  roughly chopped

FOR THE FISH
finely grated zest of
  ½ a lime
1½ tsp chilli/chili
  powder
1 egg, any size
about 30 g/1 oz. panko
  crumbs (3 handfuls)
200 g/7 oz. boneless,
  skinless firm white
  fish fillets
2 tbsp oil
4–6 small corn tortillas,
  warmed in a pan
  or microwave
lime wedges, to serve
  (optional)

1 For the *pico de gallo*, halve the tomato and, using your fingers, scoop out and discard the seeds. Chop quite finely, season with salt and put in a small sieve/strainer set over a bowl. Prepare the remaining ingredients, season again, and put on top of the tomato in the sieve. Leave to drain. Just before serving, discard the drained liquid and mix the tomato and other ingredients.

2 For the pickled radishes, mix the ingredients together and set aside. Just before serving, drain in a small sieve and check the seasoning.

3 Whizz the *crema* ingredients in a small food processor till smooth and a flecked pale green, season generously and transfer to a small bowl.

4 For the fish, mix the zest, 1 teaspoon of the chilli powder, the egg and seasoning in a shallow dish, and the panko crumbs and remaining ½ teaspoon chilli powder in another. Cut the fish into 6 or 8 strips. Dip each in the egg mixture and then cover with crumbs and put on a plate. Sprinkle over any remaining crumbs (discard any remaining egg mixture).

5 Heat the oil in a frying pan until shimmering, then shake each piece of fish gently to remove the excess crumbs and fry for 1–3 minutes on each side, depending on size, till golden and cooked through.

6 Lay out the warm tortillas and top with the fish, radishes, *crema*, *pico de gallo* and lime wedges for squeezing. Roll up and tuck in. *¡Buen provecho!*

Indian butter chicken with palak aloo

I love to transform my kitchen on a Friday evening into an imaginary Indian bazaar, with fragrant spices filling the air. One of my most treasured cookbooks dates back to 1982 – Madhur Jaffrey's Indian Cookery – and you can see from its state that I have cooked practically every recipe in it. My palak aloo is an adaptation of Madhur's recipe, which includes mustard seeds, rather than cumin seeds which are more commonly found in this North Indian recipe. This meal involves quite a few ingredients, so take your time and relax over it. If you have a bag of mini poppadoms to eat as you cook, they will help the time fly. Serve with fluffy basmati rice, mango chutney and poppadoms.

1 Mix the chicken pieces in a bowl with 2 tablespoons of the cream and set aside while you make the *palak aloo*.

2 Cook all but a handful of the spinach in a medium pan (one with a lid) with a pinch of salt and stir over a high heat till wilted. Drain in a colander (no need to wash the pan) and chop roughly.

3 Now heat the ghee in the same pan and add the asafoetida and mustard seeds. Cook until you hear the seeds begin to pop, then add the onion and garlic and cook for 1 minute, then add the potatoes and cayenne. Turn them around till hot and sizzling, then add the spinach, 3 tablespoons of water and seasoning. Turn the heat to low, cover and cook for 20–25 minutes, checking the mixture is at a very low simmer. Add a little extra water if the pan is looking dry, or if it is looking wet towards the end, remove the lid to boil away excess moisture. When the potatoes are tender, turn off the heat, check the seasoning, cover and keep warm.

4 For the chicken, preheat the grill/broiler to high. Heat the ghee in a medium saucepan (one with a lid). Now add the next 4 ingredients and fry till softened and golden, about 8 minutes. Add the spices and sugar and cook for 2 minutes. Stir in the tomatoes and seasoning. Bring to the boil, then transfer to a small food processor. Whizz till smooth, add the remaining cream and whizz again. Put back in the pan, check the seasoning, cover and keep warm.

5 Line your grill/broiler pan with foil for easy clean-up and arrange the chicken pieces in a layer on the rack. Grill for about 10 minutes, turning with tongs at half time. The chicken should be cooked through and beginning to char (if you have a digital thermometer, it should read 75°C/167°F). Stir into the creamy sauce. Serve the chicken sprinkled with almonds, along with the *palak aloo* (into which you have stirred the remaining spinach leaves to brighten the colour) and rice. Accompany with poppadoms and chutney, if liked.

FOR THE CHICKEN

- 2 or 3 chicken thigh fillets, (250 g/9 oz. total weight) sliced into 2-cm/¾-in. pieces
- 175 ml/6 fl oz./¾ cup double/heavy cream
- 1 tbsp ghee
- ½ an onion, chopped
- 3 garlic cloves, crushed
- 3-cm/1¼-in. piece of fresh ginger, finely chopped
- 1 fresh red or green chilli/chile, chopped
- 2 tsp garam masala (see Trick of the Trade, page 67)
- ½ tsp each ground coriander, cumin and turmeric
- 1 tsp sugar
- 230-g/8-oz. can chopped tomatoes, or ½ a 400-g/14-oz. can
- toasted flaked/slivered almonds, to garnish

FOR THE PALAK ALOO

- 250 g/9 oz. fresh spinach
- 1 tbsp ghee
- a pinch of ground asafoetida
- 1 tsp black or brown mustard seeds
- ½ onion, thinly sliced
- 1 garlic clove, crushed
- 1 or 2 potatoes (about 150-g/5½ oz.), peeled and cut into 2-cm/¾-in. cubes
- a good shake of cayenne pepper

Pizza nite

You have probably watched pizzaiolas at work, spinning balls of dough into thin discs, nonchalantly throwing on sauce and toppings and sliding them into the furnace – all the while sharing jokes with the other chefs and singing snatches of Italian opera.

With a little organization, you can transform your kitchen into a pizzeria for the evening. You don't need any special equipment except a rimless baking tray or sheet – and La Traviata playing in the background.

One of the things I like about making pizza from scratch is that the timings are relaxed. It's not like baking a loaf of bread, where success or failure depends on catching the dough at the right moment. Apart from the initial proving (about an hour), you can take the stretching and assembling at your own speed, then whack the pizzas into your 'furnace' when hunger strikes.

FOR TWO MEDIUM PIZZAS
250-g/8¾ oz./1¾ cups strong white/bread flour, plus extra for dusting
¾ tsp salt
1 tsp instant dried yeast, or ½ a 7-g/¼-oz. sachet
1 tsp olive oil, plus a little extra
up to 150 ml/5 fl oz./⅔ cup hand-hot water

FOR THE MARGHERITA SAUCE
230-g/8-oz. can chopped tomatoes, or ½ a 400-g/14-oz. can
2 tsp olive oil
1 small garlic clove, crushed
½ tsp dried oregano
¼ tsp crushed chilli/hot red pepper flakes
a pinch of sugar
125-g/4½-oz. mozzarella ball, drained
3 tbsp grated Parmesan
a few pitted black olives, salami slices, pine nuts, and any other toppings of your choice
a handful of fresh basil leaves, torn, to garnish

1 Start the dough in plenty of time. Put the flour, salt and yeast in the bowl of a small food processor and pulse to mix. With the machine running, add the oil, then slowly pour in most of the water and watch amazed as it forms into a dough. Continue to process for 2–3 minutes, lifting the dough out every 20–30 seconds to give it a rough knead. Flour varies, so add a little more water if necessary to achieve a soft, yielding, pliable dough. (It's better to hold back on the water than add too much, then have to add more flour.) Once you are satisfied, knead briefly in your hands, till smooth, then roll about in a medium bowl with a little more oil, cover the bowl with plastic film and leave to rise somewhere warm for 1 hour. In cold weather, I turn on my oven light (not the actual oven) and put the dough in there. When the dough has doubled in size, it is ready to use, or you can put it in the fridge for 1–2 hours, or even overnight, if convenient.

2 About 30 minutes before eating, preheat the oven to 230°C fan/250°C/500°F and slide in 2 oven shelves. Turn the dough onto a floured surface, divide into 2 pieces (about 200 g/7 oz. each) and pull and stretch each half into a taut ball. Leave on the work surface covered with plastic film while you prepare the sauce and toppings.

3 For the tomato sauce, pulse the tomatoes and their juice in a small food processor with the oil, garlic, oregano, chilli flakes and sugar until it is as smooth or chunky as you prefer. Taste for seasoning, adding enough salt to round out the flavour. Transfer to a small bowl. Shred the mozzarella onto a piece of kitchen paper towel, to blot away the excess moisture.

4 When ready to cook, cut 2 pieces of baking parchment, each about 30-cm/11¾-inch square and flour lightly. One ball at a time, stretch and

press the dough on a piece of parchment paper to form a disc as big as you can, flicking a little extra flour underneath as necessary, then cover each piece of dough with plastic film and use a rolling pin. The dough will try to shrink back, so give it time, moving from one piece of dough to the other, and taking the odd break. Aim for about 25 cm/9¾ inches in diameter – smaller will result in a thicker pizza, larger in a thinner and crispier one.

5 Top each pizza with ½ the tomato sauce, ½ the mozzarella, ½ the Parmesan and any other toppings you are using. Slide a rimless baking tray or sheet under the first pizza (still on its parchment) and then slide the pizza (yes, still on its parchment) directly onto one of the oven shelves. Repeat with the other. Once each pizza is puffed and the cheese is melty – 9–10 minutes – hoik it out (use tongs or your fingers to grab the corner of the parchment and pull it onto the baking tray or sheet), slide onto a wooden board, discard the parchment, cut into wedges with a pizza wheel (if you have one), scatter over a few basil leaves to finish and tuck in.

Cheeseburger heaven with oven onion rings

I am a proud Anglo-American, having been born in the United States to British parents who emigrated there after the war. My mother adopted the American way of life with gusto, and wrote home describing all the wonderful things she was cooking, thanks to unlimited supplies of sugar, butter, cream and bacon. Her family in England – still rationed – went into agonies of jealousy and resentment, and never truly found it in their hearts to forgive her. I sometimes think of this as the British-American problem, in microcosm.

For a treat, my mother would sometimes make us hamburgers. They weren't as exciting as TV dinners – how could they be? – but they still felt very special.

In my method, the cheese is in the middle of the burger, and it's accompanied by burger sauce and crunchy oven onion rings (which are – honestly – every bit as good as deep-fried). To complete the meal, all you need is a pair of burger buns – I love the 'brioche-style' ones that are now available – split and lightly toasted – and a good tangy coleslaw on the side, of course.

1 Mix the burger sauce ingredients, taste for seasoning and refrigerate till ready to serve.

2 *For the oven onion rings*, whizz the biscuits in a small food processor, or put in a food bag and bash into powder with a rolling pin, and mix with the panko crumbs. Make a production line of flour, egg and panko mixture. Put the onion rings in the flour and use a spoon to dust them all over, then 2-by-2, coat them in egg, then crumbs. Put on a plate as you go along, then when finished, tip any leftover crumbs over the rings and refrigerate. When ready to cook, line a rimmed baking tray or sheet large enough for the onions with baking parchment (for easy clean-up) and pour over the oil. Heat in the oven at 200°C fan/220°C/450°F. When the oil is hot, lift the onion rings off the plate, shaking off the excess crumbs, and place on the baking tray, then bake for 15 minutes, turning over at half time. These are best eaten at once, but can be kept hot till ready.

3 Fry the bacon in a medium frying pan till crisp and wrinkled – 2–5 minutes. Transfer to a plate, cut each rasher in half and keep warm. If you have fat in the pan (bacon varies), transfer it to a bowl, along with any browned bits. No need to wash the pan, which you will use again in step 5.

4 While the bacon is frying, soak the bread in the milk for 5 minutes, then mash to a smooth paste. Crush in the garlic, add the salt and use a fork to mash together. Now form the hamburgers, which requires a light touch. Break the minced beef into the bowl with the bacon fat, and add the bread mixture and plenty of pepper. Using your hands, work gently together until everything is mixed and the meat just holds together.

FOR THE BURGER SAUCE
- 2 tbsp mayonnaise
- 2 tbsp tomato ketchup
- 2 tsp American or Dijon mustard
- 1 tsp pickle relish, or finely chopped dill pickle or gherkin

FOR THE OVEN ONION RINGS
- 5 or 6 cheese biscuits/crackers or Ritz crackers (25 g/1 oz.)
- 4 tbsp panko crumbs
- 3 tbsp flour, plus extra for dusting
- 1 egg, any size, beaten
- 8–10 rings, cut from 1 large onion
- 2 tbsp oil

FOR THE CHEESEBURGERS
- 4 rashers/slices of bacon
- 1 slice of white bread, crusts removed, crumbled
- 2 tbsp milk
- 1 garlic clove
- ½ tsp salt
- 350 g/12 oz./3¼ cups best quality minced/ground beef
- 25-g/1 oz./¼ cup grated Gruyère or Cheddar
- 1 tbsp oil

TRICK OF THE TRADE

*Do you have a **mincer/meat grinder**? I bought an inexpensive one a couple of years ago and once I conquered how to assemble it (and even harder, how to get it back in its box to store it) I haven't looked back. For a de luxe burger, sirloin makes the best mince.*

Form into 4 equal balls (about 85 g/3 oz. each) and flatten each on a lightly floured board to form a disc about 1 cm/⅜ inch thick and 9 cm/3½ inches across. Arrange half the grated cheese on each disc, leaving a narrow border around the edge, then top with the remaining discs to sandwich the cheese. Pinch gently around the edges to seal. Flatten the burgers, making a shallow indentation in the top of each with the palm of your hand (this helps keep the shape when frying). Dust the burgers with a little flour and refrigerate on a plate till ready to cook.

5 Heat the oil in the frying pan till shimmering and add the burgers. Cook for about 4 minutes, then flip for another 3. Once they are cooked to your liking, they can wait in the oven for a few minutes if convenient. Serve in burger buns, topped with sauce and bacon, plus a side of onion rings.

Cowboy chilli with all the fixin's

To make a proper chilli, which will put others in the shade, prepare your own spice mix, slow-simmer the meat till it is richly caramelized and lay on all the accompaniments. This is best made the day before, to let the flavours meld.

Chilli is often made with minced/ground meat, but cutting braising steak into small chunks gives a more satisfying texture. On the subject of texture, canned black beans make an interesting change from red kidney beans, although these are not available in handy 230-g/8-oz. cans.

I am not keen on very spicy food because I find the heat cancels out all the other flavours, but feel free to dial up the any of the chilli elements. If one of you likes this hotter than the other, you can always adjust things further at the table with a sprinkling of Tabasco.

1 Mix the spices and oregano in a small bowl. Heat the oil in a medium frying pan (one with a lid) and brown the bacon and meat, sizzling, for 5 minutes, till well browned, then add the onion and jalapeño for 3–4 minutes, till beginning to colour. Add the garlic and spice mix and cook for 1 minute (it will look sticky), then add the canned tomatoes, chilli flakes and sugar and enough water just to cover. (This depends on the size of your pan, but I use the empty tomato can as a measure, and ½–¾ of a can of water does it.)

2 Bring to the boil and put on the lid. Either cook on the hob/stovetop at a low simmer for 1 hour, or if your pan and lid are ovenproof, you can put in the oven at 130°C fan/150°C/300°F for 1¼–1½ hours. Stir occasionally, and halfway through, season to taste, and if you wish, up the heat by adding more chilli flakes. If you prefer a more saucy chilli, add a splash more water, or remove the lid if you like it thicker. When the meat is totally tender and can be mashed with a fork, and you have achieved your desired consistency, stir in the kidney beans and simmer for 5 minutes, then stir in the chocolate to melt, and either serve with accompaniments, or look forward to a feast tomorrow.

FOR THE SPICE MIX
½–1 tsp chilli/chili powder
½ tsp cumin seeds
½ tsp smoked paprika
½ tsp dried oregano

FOR THE MEAT
1 tbsp oil
1 or 2 rashers/slices of smoked bacon, thinly sliced, or 40 g/1½ oz. /⅓ cup lardons
200 g/7 oz. braising beef/chuck steak, sliced into 1–2-cm/ ⅜–¾-in. chunks
1 small onion, thinly sliced
½–1 fresh jalapeño chilli/chile, thinly sliced
1 garlic clove, sliced
230-g/8-oz. can chopped tomatoes, or ½ a 400-g/14-oz. can

½ tsp sugar
a pinch of crushed Ancho chilli flakes, or regular chilli/hot red pepper flakes, plus more to taste
230-g/8-oz. can red kidney beans, drained and rinsed
a small square of dark/ bittersweet chocolate

FOR THE FIXIN'S
all or any of these, to serve:
tortilla chips
cooked plain or Mexican-style rice
shredded spring onions/ scallions
diced avocado
soured cream
crumbled feta or grated Cheddar
lime wedges
Tabasco

Homage to Peking duck

This is fun to make, with vibrant flavours and textures. Much has been written about how to achieve an authentic Peking duck, with lacquered skin and shreddy texture. It is a crowning achievement of the chef's art, but a huge undertaking for the amateur. If it sounds your kind of challenge, and you have an electric bicycle pump, a fan, an outhouse and a couple of days to spare, you'll find lots of advice online (along with how to deep-fry a 20-lb. turkey in a 40-quart oil barrel). In this recipe, I salt, slow-roast and shred regular duck breasts, while dreaming of Chinatown. The salting needs to be started well ahead.

In Beijing, I am told the fashion is to serve Peking duck with strips of melon, alongside the cucumber and spring onions/scallions: I love this idea. (If you don't want to buy a whole melon, you can buy a tub of prepared fruit salad and use the melon from that.)

FOR THE DUCK
2 duck legs
a sprinkle of five-spice powder
a drizzle of runny honey

FOR THE FRUITY HOISIN SAUCE
5 tbsp hoisin sauce
2 spring onions/scallions, very thinly sliced
1-cm/³∕₈-in. piece of fresh ginger, grated
a little grated orange zest
a little grated garlic
1 tsp Chinese vinegar or wine vinegar
a pinch each of five-spice powder and crushed chilli/hot red pepper flakes

FOR THE CHINESE PANCAKES
110 g/4 oz./¾ cup plus 1½ tbsp flour, plus extra for dusting
90 ml/3 fl oz./⅓ cup boiling water
a splash of toasted sesame oil
a splash of oil

TO SERVE
½ cucumber, cut into batons
4 spring onions/scallions, shredded
6 thin strips of melon
soy sauce

1 Dry the duck with kitchen paper towels and put on a plate. Rub with plenty of salt and the five-spice, then put in the fridge, uncovered, for 12 hours or overnight.

2 Jazz up the bought hoisin sauce by stirring in the extra ingredients listed and set aside till ready.

3 To cook the duck, pat the legs dry, put in a small frying pan, turn on the heat and fry for 5 minutes on each side, till nicely browned. Transfer to a small roasting tin or pan, brush over the honey and roast at 180°C fan/200°C/400°F for 20 minutes, then turn the oven down to 120°C fan/140°C/280°F for 1 further hour, or until the meat is soft. Allow to rest for 5–10 minutes, then shred the duck meat and skin. While the duck is in the oven, make the pancakes.

4 **To make the Chinese pancakes**, mix the flour and a big pinch of salt in a heatproof bowl and pour in the boiling water. Mix with a spatula to form a sticky dough (don't panic – it looks terrible at first) and when cool enough to touch – 3–4 minutes – knead for 5 minutes on a lightly floured surface, till smooth. If it is too sticky to handle – flour varies – add more flour, 1 teaspoonful at a time. Cover in plastic film and leave on the work surface for ½–1 hour.

5 Shape the pancakes by rolling the dough into a log and cutting into 6 pieces (about 30-g/1 oz. each). Roll each into a ball, then squash it under your palm to make a disc about 6 cm/2½ inches in diameter. Take 3 of these discs and brush the tops and sides with sesame oil. Put 1 unoiled disc on top of each oiled disc, to form 3 double deckers. Take 1 and roll it out on a lightly floured work surface, turning over frequently, to form a 17-cm/6¾-inch circle. Repeat with the remaining 2.

6 Heat the oil in a frying pan till shimmering, then wipe out with a piece of kitchen paper towel. Put the first pancake in the pan and watch as – after 30–40 seconds – you see it puff in places. Peek underneath the pancake – it should be white with a few pale brown patches – and flip for another 30 seconds (more puffing). Slide onto a plate, wait 30 seconds, then gently separate the upper and lower pancake. Stack, spotty-side down, and continue with the remaining pancakes. Keep warm, covered with plastic film, or reheat in the microwave on high for 30 seconds just before serving.

7 To enjoy, take a pancake, spread with fruity hoisin sauce, then load with duck, cucumber, spring onions, melon and a sprinkle of soy sauce. Fold in the bottom and sides of the pancake to form a wrap, and eat with your hands. Repeat with the remaining pancakes.

Southern fried chicken & buttermilk biscuits

As they know in the American South, there ain't no beatin' home-fried chicken. It's the sort of dish which is stressful to make for a crowd, but for two – pure fun.

A few pointers. I am always going on about digital thermometers, but I would specially recommend one for deep-frying. Otherwise, check the oil is hot enough by dipping in the handle of a wooden spoon: it should be immediately surrounded by bubbles which float up. If it bubbles hard, the oil is too hot. Note also that the chicken is deep-fried, then transferred to the oven to finish cooking. This gives a useful interlude for clearing up, though the cooking oil is best left till tomorrow (and disposed of, as it will be too dark and murky for further use).

Traditional accompaniments are 'biscuits' (very similar to British scones), gravy (thick and chickeny), mashed potatoes (include a splash of any leftover buttermilk) and green beans.

1 Mix the spice ingredients in a small bowl.

2 Mix the buttermilk, egg yolk, salt and 2 teaspoons of the spice mixture in a bowl large enough to hold the chicken pieces. Add the chicken and spoon the buttermilk mixture over to coat completely. Cover and refrigerate for 6 hours or longer, stirring the contents of the bowl occasionally.

3 *For the buttermilk biscuits,* line a baking tray or sheet with baking parchment. Sprinkle your work surface lightly with a little flour, and stand a 6-cm/2½-inch cutter in a small bowl of flour. Mix the buttermilk and milk, and have a little extra milk standing by just in case. Mix the flour, sugar and salt in a separate bowl, sprinkle the butter over, then rub in using your fingertips, lifting high to keep the mixture light. Shake the bowl to bring any lumps to the top and repeat.

4 Pour most of the buttermilk mixture over the flour, then gently and patiently work together using a table knife until it forms a soft but not sticky dough. Work in any loose dry bits of mixture, adding the remaining buttermilk and a dash of extra milk if necessary. Do not overwork. Knead the dough 3 or 4 times to bring it together and roll out until it is 2.5-cm/1-inch thick. Use the floured cutter to stamp out rounds cleanly and without twisting and place on the lined baking tray. Gather and re-roll the scraps to make 1 more biscuit, then discard the remaining dough. Brush the

FOR THE SPICE MIXTURE
2 tsp paprika
2 tsp ground black pepper
⅔ tsp chilli/chili powder
⅔ tsp dried oregano
½ tsp garlic granules (optional)

FOR THE MARINADE
75 ml/2½ fl oz./⅓ cup buttermilk
1 egg yolk, any size
1 tsp salt
4 chicken thighs (with skin and bone), or 2 chicken legs (with skin and bone), each cut into 2 (drumstick and thigh)

FOR THE CRUST
75 g/2¾ oz./½ cup plus 1 tbsp flour
20 g/3 tbsp cornflour/cornstarch
1 tsp salt
½ tsp baking powder
1 litre/4 generous cups oil or corn oil, for deep frying
flaky salt, to sprinkle

FOR THE BUTTERMILK BISCUITS
a little flour, for sprinkling and shaping
125 ml/4 fl oz./½ cup buttermilk
4 tbsp milk, plus a little extra
225 g/8 oz./1¾ cups self-raising/rising flour, or use 225 g/8 oz./1¾ cups plain/all-purpose flour plus 2 tsp baking powder
2 tsp sugar
¼ tsp salt
50 g/3½ tbsp butter, cut into 1-cm/³⁄₈-cubes cubes, plus extra for serving

tops with a little milk then bake at 200°C fan/220°C/450°F for 12–15 minutes, rotating the baking tray at half time, until the biscuits are risen and golden. Cool on a wire rack.

5 To coat the chicken, mix the flour, cornflour, salt, baking powder and remaining spice mixture in a large, wide bowl. Mix in 1 tablespoon of the buttermilk marinade using a fork. Lift out the first chicken piece with your fingers and let the marinade drip off, then place in the flour mixture and spoon flour over it to coat. Repeat with the remaining pieces, then gently move the chicken pieces about, pressing the flour on to ensure everything is thickly coated. Set the bowl aside, or refrigerate if not cooking immediately.

6 Heat the oil in a large, deep saucepan to 180°C/356°F. (If it gets too hot, allow it to cool before frying.) When ready, lift the first piece of chicken and shake gently over the bowl to remove excess flour, then use tongs, a slotted spoon or skimmer to lower it gently into the hot oil. Don't worry if it isn't fully submerged. Repeat with the remaining pieces. Do not touch the chicken for 1½ minutes, then use tongs to peek underneath. When the bottom has developed a rich golden crust, flip for 1½ minutes longer, then flip again for 1½ minutes. Transfer to a small roasting tin or pan and bake at 160°C fan/180°C/350°F oven for 10–15 minutes to finish cooking. If you have a digital thermometer, the thickest part of the chicken should read 75°C/167°F. Sprinkle with a little flaky salt and serve the chicken in all its crusty glory, along with the biscuits, split and buttered, and other accompaniments of your choice.

Thai feast

This meal is a celebration of Thai flavours. It is meat-free and can easily be adapted for vegans (simply omit the egg and use an alternative to fish sauce), but does rely on hunting out a handful of authentic ingredients. It is a generous spread, organised into three straightforward steps. If you're not that hungry, make just the butternut squash curry and rice, or just the pad Thai.

One ingredient I find impossible to buy in practical quantities is beansprouts. I have thrown so many quarter-used packs over the years that nowadays I prefer to add crunch with chopped celery instead, or roughly chopped crisp lettuce stirred in right at the end.

1 For the butternut squash curry, heat the oil in a medium or large frying pan and fry the onion gently for 3 minutes, till transparent but not brown. Add the garlic, ginger and curry paste and sizzle for 1 minute, till sticky. Add the remaining ingredients and simmer together, covered, until the squash is tender, 15–20 minutes. Check the seasoning and set aside for now.

2 For the jasmine rice, stir the ingredients together in a medium pan. Bring to the boil, stirring often, and simmer, covered, for 15 minutes, stirring occasionally, till the liquid has been absorbed. Leave for 10 minutes, or longer if convenient, and fluff before serving.

3 For the pad Thai, if using dried noodles, cook following the pack instructions, drain and leave in cold water to prevent sticking. Whisk the sugar, tamarind, fish sauce and lime juice in a small bowl. Dry the tofu on a piece of kitchen paper towel, put in a bowl, sprinkle with the cornflour and toss gently to coat. Fry the tofu in 1 tablespoon of oil until crisp and browned – 2–3 minutes – and set aside. Add a little extra oil if necessary and sizzle the shallot, garlic and chilli until beginning to soften (about 30 seconds), then push to the side of the pan and pour in the egg, moving it about to scramble. Add the tamarind mixture, tofu and remaining ingredients to the pan to heat through. If using lettuce, add at the last minute.

4 Serve the 3 dishes together, strewing the squash curry with basil leaves and sprinkling the pad Thai with chopped peanuts, along with soy sauce for drizzling and lime wedges at the side for squeezing.

FOR THE BUTTERNUT
SQUASH CURRY
1 tbsp oil
1 small onion, sliced
2 garlic cloves, crushed
2-cm/¾-in. piece of
    fresh ginger, grated
2 tbsp Thai red curry
    paste
⅔ a 400-g/14-oz. can
    coconut milk
3 tbsp ground almonds
½ a 400-g/14-oz. can
    chickpeas, drained
    and rinsed
½ a small butternut
    squash, cut into
    2-cm/¾-in. cubes
    (200–250 g/7–9 oz.
    prepared weight)
a small handful of fresh
    Thai basil leaves, torn,
    to garnish

FOR THE JASMINE RICE
100 g/3½ oz./heaping
    ½ cup jasmine rice
⅓ a 400-g/14-oz. can
    coconut milk
120 ml/4 fl oz./½ cup
    water
1 tsp sugar
¼ tsp salt

FOR THE PAD THAI
140 g/5 oz. fresh rice
    noodles, or 100 g/
    3½ oz. dried medium
    rice noodles
1 tbsp sugar
1 tbsp tamarind paste
1 tbsp fish sauce, or
    vegan substitute
juice of ¼ a lime
200 g/7 oz. firm tofu,
    cut into 1-cm/⅜-in.
    cubes
1 tbsp cornflour/
    cornstarch
1 tbsp oil, plus a little
    extra
1 shallot, finely chopped
2 garlic cloves, crushed
1 fresh Thai chilli/chile,
    deseeded and very
    thinly sliced
1 egg, any size, beaten
2 spring onions/
    scallions, thinly sliced
a small handful of fresh
    coriander/cilantro,
    chopped
a handful of fresh
    beansprouts, sliced
    celery, or chopped
    crisp lettuce
chopped dry roasted
    peanuts, soy sauce
    and lime wedges,
    to serve

SATURDAY NIGHT SPECIALS

I spend all week looking forward to Saturday evening, when I am in the mood to cook something mouthwateringly special. All these recipes come with a flourish, and all of them have been created to serve two.

Cassoulet du jour

Battles have been fought in South West France over which is the 'authentic' cassoulet – that of Castelnaudary, Toulouse or Carcassonne – but all agree that, in essence, it is a bean stew enriched with tasty scraps of meat. You can spend several days making it – first slaughter your pig – or you can put it together quickly, taking advantage of convenient canned and preserved ingredients. Apart from heating the confit, my version is cooked in one pan.

In France, this dish is served 'soupy', with lots of tawny liquid to spoon or soak up with bread. If you prefer it thicker, more like a stew (as I do), then reduce it to your desired consistency in step 3.

Confit duck legs can be bought easily nowadays from supermarket chillers or in cans. They are by definition a product that keeps well, so as you only need one for this recipe, refrigerate or freeze any extra for next time.

Even if you wouldn't find them in an authentic cassoulet served in a country auberge, pork scratchings – that favourite old-fashioned British pub snack – make a crunchy topping for this dish, and I hope the excellent folk of the Midi-Pyrenées and Languedoc will approve.

1 confit duck leg

a knob/pat of butter

2 tbsp olive oil

1 slice of white bread, crusts removed, roughly cubed

2 Toulouse sausages (about 130 g/4½ oz.)

50 g/1¾ oz./⅓ cup lardons

1 red onion, chopped (see Trick of the Trade)

2 garlic cloves, crushed

230-g/8-oz. can chopped tomatoes, or ½ a 400-g/ 14-oz. can

200 ml/6¾ fl oz./¾ cup chicken stock

100 ml/3⅓ fl oz./⅓ cup plus 1 tbsp white or red wine

a 20-cm/8-in. fresh rosemary sprig

1 tsp Dijon mustard

400-g/14-oz. can cannellini beans, drained and rinsed

15 g/½ oz./scant ¼ cup pork scratchings (1 small handful) roughly chopped, to finish (optional)

1 Cook the confit duck according to the pack instructions (typically, 25–30 minutes in a 200°C fan/220°C/450°F oven). Heat the butter and ½ the oil in a large frying pan (one with a lid) and fry the bread cubes until toasty, about 5 minutes. Transfer to a small dish.

2 Add the remaining oil to the pan and fry the sausages for 5 minutes, turning often, till brown. Remove to a plate.

3 Add the lardons and onion to the pan and fry for 4 minutes, until brown, then add the garlic for 1 minute. Stir in the tomatoes and their juices. Add the stock, wine, rosemary sprig, mustard and beans and bring to a simmer. Cook for 10–15 minutes, uncovered, till the sauce reaches your desired thickness, then discard the rosemary skeleton.

4 While the mixture simmers, use a knife and fork to cut the sausage then into chunks and the duck into bite-size pieces. Add to the simmering mixture for a further 5 minutes, covered, till all is hot and the sausage is cooked through.

5 Set aside for a full 10 minutes, to allow the cassoulet to cool slightly and the flavours to meld, before serving sprinkled with the fried bread cubes and pork scratchings, if using.

TRICK OF THE TRADE

*I haven't spent time **chopping onions** for 20 years – the day I bought an Alligator chopper. This remarkable gadget, made in Sweden, is one of my desert island gadgets: it turns vegetables into small, even dice with one swift karate chop.*

Chicken saltimbocca with crushed herby potatoes & courgettes

The Italians have a poetic touch when it comes to naming dishes – saltimbocca means literally 'jump in the mouth'. Crisp sage leaves add a pretty finish to this dish, and yes, they are meant to be eaten. The green vegetable can be varied according to the season.

1 Pick out the 4–6 most handsome sage leaves, and chop the rest finely. While you are at it, chop the other herbs. If you are making the potatoes, chop the herbs for these now too, and set aside separately. Slice each chicken breast in half horizontally, to form 4 escalopes, cover with a sheet of plastic film, and bash each with a rolling pin until they are an even 1 cm/³⁄₈ inch thick. Dab the escalopes dry with a piece of kitchen paper towel, season all over with salt and pepper and sprinkle the cut sides with ½ the chopped sage. Press the Prosciutto slices on the cut, sage-flecked sides, tucking the edges under on themselves to follow the shape. Put on a plate and refrigerate.

2 **For the crushed herby potatoes**, put them in a small pan, add water to cover by about 2 cm/¾ inch, salt generously and boil for 12–15 minutes, until soft but not falling apart. Drain. Put the butter into the pan plus the chopped herbs and seasoning, then stir in the potatoes, squashing each one lightly with a wooden spoon or spatula so it breaks up and absorbs the buttery herbs, but without mashing. Check the seasoning, cover and keep warm. Cook the courgette batons in a pan of salted, boiling water till just tender – 3–5 minutes depending on size – then drain and keep warm.

3 Heat the oil in a large frying pan and when shimmering, add the sage leaves. Cook for just 30–40 seconds till they darken and stiffen, then transfer with tongs to a small plate lined with kitchen paper towels. Sprinkle with salt and set aside. Now add the chicken to the pan, Prosciutto-side down. Cook for 2 minutes until a narrow white line appears around the top edge, check the underneath is bronzed, then flip over for 2 minutes to cook through. Transfer to a plate and keep warm.

4 Add the garlic and remaining sage to the frying pan and sizzle for 30 seconds until fragrant, then pour in the stock. Bubble the sauce for 3–5 minutes until reduced by about ½ and slightly thickened. Reduce the heat and whisk in the butter in 2 pieces, then when it has melted, add lemon juice and seasoning to taste. Swirl in the courgettes.

5 Use tongs to arrange the seasoned courgettes on plates, top with the saltimboccas, drizzle with sauce and top each with a few crisp sage leaves. Serve the potatoes alongside.

about 12 fresh sage leaves
a small handful of other fresh herbs, such as parsley and chives
2 chicken breast fillets, skinless and boneless
4 Prosciutto Crudo slices
250 g/9 oz./1¾ cups small red or white potatoes, scrubbed and halved (about 2 handfuls)
25 g/2 tbsp butter
1 tbsp olive oil
1 courgette/zucchini, cut into batons, or a 150-g/5½-oz. bunch of fine asparagus, or green beans, trimmed
1 garlic clove, thinly sliced
200 ml/6¾ fl oz./¾ cup chicken stock, dry vermouth or white wine, or a mixture
about 2 tsp lemon juice

FOR THE CRUSHED HERBY POTATOES
250 g/9 oz./1¾ cups small red or white potatoes, scrubbed and halved (about 2 handfuls)
25 g/2 tbsp butter
a small handful of fresh herbs, such as parsley and chives, chopped

Couscous 'Arabian Nights'

My partner is an American academic, and a world authority on the Arabian Nights. This vegetable feast is dedicated to him. (He's also a world authority on Sweeney Todd, but that's for another day.) You can vary this dish in a thousand-and-one ways, according to what vegetables catch your eye. If you shop in a supermarket, check out the small 'variety packs' of veg and baby veg, which are ideal for this dish. You might also wish to raid your freezer. As well as obvious things like peas and leaf spinach, I keep a supply of sweetcorn/corn kernels and prepared butternut squash there. You can add a handful of frozen sweetcorn in step 2, and squash in step 3.

a pinch of saffron threads
1 tsp each ground cinnamon,
    cumin and turmeric
1 tsp paprika
½–1 tsp crushed chilli/hot red
    pepper flakes (to taste)
couscous, to serve
a handful of chopped fresh
    herbs
1–2 tsp harissa paste
a squeeze of lemon juice
toasted flaked/slivered almonds,
    to finish

FOR THE GREEN VEGETABLES
3 Brussels sprouts, quartered
1 small leek, trimmed and thinly
    sliced
a handful of French green
    beans, halved
a handful of broccoli, trimmed
    into small florets
a handful of frozen peas
    (no need to defrost)

FOR THE RED VEGETABLES
1 tbsp olive oil
1 red onion, thinly sliced
1 carrot, cut into thin strips
½ red (bell) pepper, deseeded
    and thinly sliced
2 garlic cloves, thinly sliced
400-g/14-oz. can chopped
    tomatoes
4 dried organic apricots, sliced
    (see Trick of the Trade)
½ a 400-g/14-oz. can chickpeas

1 Crumble the saffron into a dry pan and heat till fragrant and beginning to darken (1–2 minutes) then transfer to a small bowl and cover with 100 ml/3⅓ fl oz./⅓ cup plus 1 tbsp boiling water. Leave to infuse.

2 Blanch the fresh green vegetables (not the frozen peas) by bringing a medium pan of well-salted water to the boil, and cooking till tender (about 5 minutes). Drain, cool quickly under running water for 1 minute, then tip into a large bowl of cold water. Add the frozen peas and 3 or 4 ice cubes, to 'shock' the vegetables and keep them bright green.

3 Now heat the oil in the saucepan and fry the onion, carrot and pepper for 5 minutes, till softened. Add the garlic for 30 seconds, then ¾ of the tomatoes, the apricots and the saffron water, plus the cinnamon, cumin, paprika, turmeric and crushed chilli flakes. Bring to the boil and simmer, covered, for 20 minutes, till everything is tender. Drain the chickpeas and add them to the mixture (no need to rinse), along with the drained green vegetables. Heat through and add more tomatoes if you like it more saucy. Cook 2 servings of couscous according to the pack instructions, adding the herbs and a splash of oil at the fluffing stage.

4 Before serving, taste the vegetables for seasoning. Spoon out 6–7 tablespoons of the liquid and mix in a small jug/pitcher with the harissa and lemon juice to make a spicy drizzling sauce. (I find the heat of harissa varies from brand to brand, so add more or less to taste.)

5 Serve the vegetables on a bed of couscous, sprinkled with the almonds and drizzled with the harissa sauce.

TRICK OF THE TRADE

*I can see the attraction of 'ordinary' dried apricots, because of their zingy colour, but once you have tasted **organic dried apricots** – which look less alluring but taste far sweeter and fruitier – there is no turning back. They have the added benefit of being free from sulphur dioxide...*

Coconut prawns with sriracha aïoli

Sriracha is a chilli-based dipping sauce found in Thai and Vietnamese cuisines. You only use 1–2 teaspoons for this recipe, but it is a zippy addition to one's flavour repertoire, and I keep a small jar in the fridge alongside such other flavour enhancers as gochujang and chipotle pastes, and XO sauce. Serve the prawns with plain or spiced rice, with the aïoli for dipping and lime wedges.

1 Put the prawns on a plate lined with kitchen paper towels to dry thoroughly. As described on page 115, make yourself a production line of seasoned flour in 1 shallow bowl or dish, seasoned egg in the next, and panko crumbs and coconut, mixed, in another.

2 This step requires a little patience, so put on the radio or a podcast. Patiently powder 4 prawns all over with flour, dip in egg to cover completely, then roll in the crumb mixture, pressing on firmly. Transfer to a plate and repeat with remaining prawns in batches. Put in the fridge till ready to cook.

3 *To make the sriracha aïoli*, chop then mash the garlic with a good pinch of salt, using the flat side of a chef's knife, to make a wet paste. Scrape into a small bowl set on a cloth (so it doesn't roll or slide about) and whisk together with the yolk, lime juice, pinch of sugar and more seasoning. Measure the oils into a jug/pitcher, then – whisking all the time, as if you were making mayonnaise – trickle a few drops into the egg mixture. Take a breath, add a few more drops and whisk again. Continue drizzling in the oil, as slowly as you can bear. After about ½ the oil is added, you should notice the egg mixture starting to thicken and you can go a little bit faster. When all the oil is added – it takes me 4½ minutes in total – whisk in the sriracha, taste for seasoning and serve with the prawns.

4 When ready to eat, heat the oil in a large frying pan till shimmering and add the prawns. Cook for 1½–2 minutes, swirling the pan to move them about, then use tongs to turn them over. If using raw, check they have turned from grey to pink before serving with the aïoli and lime wedges.

TRICK OF THE TRADE

*Anyone who has ever tried **making mayonnaise** at home has experienced that sinking feeling when it doesn't 'take' and you are left with a bowl of greasy yellow liquid. Like mayo, aïoli can be rescued. Start again with a fresh bowl and another egg yolk, and very gradually whisk in the failed mayo or aïoli, this time taking care to go more slowly, breathing between additions. Check the final seasoning, and if it seems too thick or eggy, add cold water, teaspoon by teaspoon, to correct.*

FOR THE COCONUT PRAWNS
150–200 g/5½–7 oz. (15–20) large peeled prawns/jumbo shrimp, cooked or raw, defrosted if frozen
2 tbsp flour
1 egg, any size, beaten
about 20 g/¾ oz. panko crumbs (2 handfuls)
about 10 g/¼ oz. desiccated coconut (1 small handful)
2 tbsp oil, for frying

FOR THE SRIRACHA AÏOLI
1 small garlic clove
1 egg yolk, any size
juice of ¼ lime
a pinch of sugar
4 tbsp oil
2 tbsp extra virgin olive oil
1–2 tsp sriracha sauce
lime wedges, to serve

Tex-mex one-pot with creamy avocado salad

This colourful and satisfying dish is a sort of Mexican pie, baked in its frying pan. If you don't have an ovenproof pan or skillet, you can transfer the filling to a shallow dish, or two individual dishes, and bake it in those. Do not be deterred by the long ingredients list – the dish comes together logically, and only takes 15 minutes in the oven.

You can make this an even more generous (and meaty) supper by frying a couple of sausages – Spanish- or Italian-style are ideal – before you start. Remove from the pan and chop into chunks before stirring back into the dish with the mozzarella.

FOR THE FILLING
1 lime
75 ml/2½ fl oz./⅓ cup milk (5 tbsp)
1 tbsp oil
3 or 4 spring onions/ scallions, sliced
½ green (bell) pepper, thinly sliced
1 tbsp tomato purée/ paste
½ small fresh green chilli/chile, finely chopped
1 garlic clove, crushed
200-g/7-oz. can chopped tomatoes, or ½ a 400-g/14-oz. can
150 g/5½ oz./1 cup frozen sweetcorn, or canned, drained
1 tsp chilli/chili powder
125-g/4½-oz. mozzarella ball, drained
a small handful of fresh coriander/cilantro, chopped
½ a 150-ml/5-fl oz. pot soured cream

FOR THE CRUST
50 g/6 tbsp self-raising/ rising flour, or use 50 g/6 tbsp plain/ all-purpose flour plus ½ tsp baking powder

¼ tsp bicarbonate of soda/baking soda
50 g/1¾ oz./⅓ cup cornmeal
2 tsp sugar
¼ tsp salt
25 g/1 oz./¼ cup grated Cheddar
15 g/1 tbsp butter, melted
1 egg, any size

FOR THE CREAMY AVOCADO SALAD
1 Little Gem lettuce
½ green (bell) pepper, thinly sliced
1 spring onion/scallion, sliced on the diagonal
a small handful of fresh coriander/cilantro, roughly chopped
1 ripe avocado
1 garlic clove, crushed
½ fresh green chilli/ chile, finely chopped
½ a 150-ml/5-fl oz. pot of soured cream
2 tbsp oil
2 tbsp mayonnaise
a splash of Tabasco
a pinch of sugar
1 tbsp grated Parmesan (optional)

1 Grate the zest of half the lime into a small bowl. Cut the lime in 2, and squeeze out 1 half. Stir 1 teaspoon of the juice into the milk, to sour it for the cornbread, and add the rest to the zest. Cut the remaining lime half into 2 segments, for serving.

2 Take a large ovenproof frying pan and heat the oil. Add the spring onions and pepper and cook over a moderate heat till golden (5–7 minutes), then stir in the tomato purée, chilli and garlic and cook for 1–2 minutes, till the purée has darkened and the garlic smells fragrant. Stir in the tomatoes and their juices, sweetcorn and chilli powder and simmer for 10 minutes, till slightly thickened. Off the heat, crumble in the mozzarella and stir in lightly along with the coriander. Put dollops of soured cream on top.

3 Mix the dry ingredients for the crust in a bowl, saving 2 tablespoons of grated Cheddar for the top. Whisk together the butter, milk (which will have curdled) and egg. Fold the two together lightly till they are just combined (a few flecks of cornmeal should still be visible) and spoon onto the vegetable mixture. Use a spatula to spread out lightly so the whole surface is roughly covered. Sprinkle with the remaining Cheddar and bake at 190°C fan/210°C/425°F for 12–15 minutes, till the crust is golden and firm.

4 *To make the creamy avocado salad*, break the lettuce up into bite-size pieces and add the green pepper, spring onion and coriander. Halve and stone the avocado, score 1 half into dice and scoop into the bowl with the lettuce. Now scoop the remaining avocado

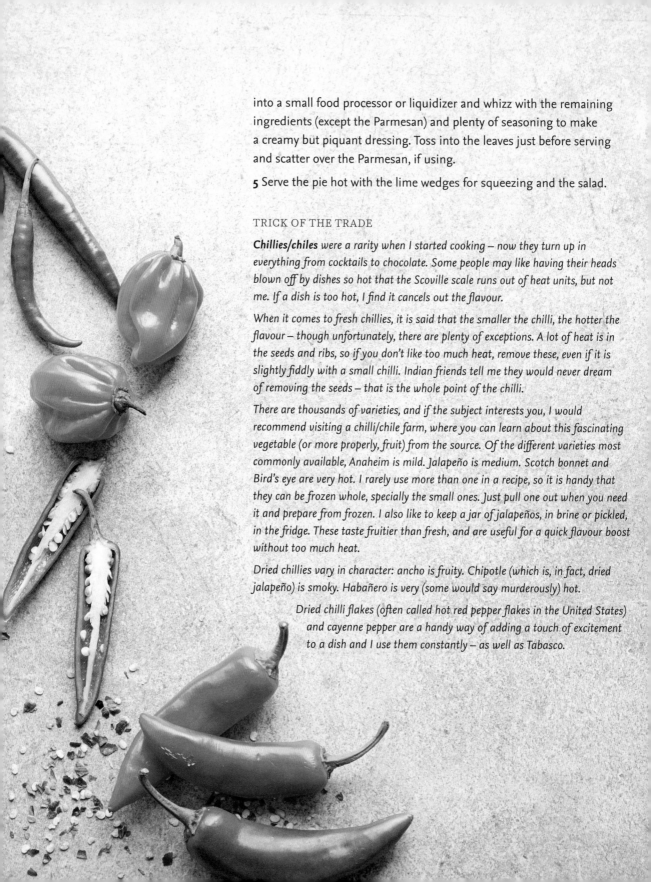

into a small food processor or liquidizer and whizz with the remaining ingredients (except the Parmesan) and plenty of seasoning to make a creamy but piquant dressing. Toss into the leaves just before serving and scatter over the Parmesan, if using.

5 Serve the pie hot with the lime wedges for squeezing and the salad.

TRICK OF THE TRADE

Chillies/chiles were a rarity when I started cooking – now they turn up in everything from cocktails to chocolate. Some people may like having their heads blown off by dishes so hot that the Scoville scale runs out of heat units, but not me. If a dish is too hot, I find it cancels out the flavour.

When it comes to fresh chillies, it is said that the smaller the chilli, the hotter the flavour – though unfortunately, there are plenty of exceptions. A lot of heat is in the seeds and ribs, so if you don't like too much heat, remove these, even if it is slightly fiddly with a small chilli. Indian friends tell me they would never dream of removing the seeds – that is the whole point of the chilli.

There are thousands of varieties, and if the subject interests you, I would recommend visiting a chilli/chile farm, where you can learn about this fascinating vegetable (or more properly, fruit) from the source. Of the different varieties most commonly available, Anaheim is mild. Jalapeño is medium. Scotch bonnet and Bird's eye are very hot. I rarely use more than one in a recipe, so it is handy that they can be frozen whole, specially the small ones. Just pull one out when you need it and prepare from frozen. I also like to keep a jar of jalapeños, in brine or pickled, in the fridge. These taste fruitier than fresh, and are useful for a quick flavour boost without too much heat.

Dried chillies vary in character: ancho is fruity. Chipotle (which is, in fact, dried jalapeño) is smoky. Habañero is very (some would say murderously) hot.

Dried chilli flakes (often called hot red pepper flakes in the United States) and cayenne pepper are a handy way of adding a touch of excitement to a dish and I use them constantly – as well as Tabasco.

Crêpes forestière

This elegant, understated dish (literally, 'forest pancakes') recalls the golden age of French cuisine, and if you enjoy a culinary challenge, is enormously rewarding to make and serve. Duxelles – mushroom stuffing – may seem a bother to make but it is worth every minute. Make sure the dish is piping hot all the way through before removing from the oven (crêpes seem to have insulating properties), then allow to cool somewhat, to prevent burning your mouth in your eagerness to tuck in.

1 Put all the crêpe ingredients in a small food processor, whizz till smooth, then transfer to a jug/pitcher. Alternatively, make 'in the old fashioned way', humming along to Charles Aznafour if you wish, by putting the dry ingredients in a bowl and gradually whisking in the liquid. Ideally, make a day ahead and refrigerate.

2 Heat a small crêpe or frying pan over a high heat and brush lightly with a little butter (it should sizzle). Make 6 crêpes in the usual way, about 18 cm/7 inches in diameter and as thin as you can. Stack them, spotty-side down, on a plate as you go (they will not stick), until you get to 6.

3 To make the duxelles, find an old, clean tea towel/dish cloth. Chop the mushrooms finely by hand (don't be tempted to put them in a processor or you will end up with a 'milled' consistency) and put a handful in the centre of the towel. Twist the towel and wring it as hard as you can over the sink, to remove excess water (which will be a surprising reddish colour), then scrape the mushrooms off the cloth into a bowl. Continue with the remaining mushrooms, then throw away the towel, or hot-wash (promptly, before it starts to ferment). Heat the butter in a large frying pan and cook the shallot for 1–2 minutes until softening, then stir in the mushrooms and cook gently for 7–8 minutes, until they are on the point of browning. Transfer to a bowl with the herbs and plenty of seasoning.

4 For the sauce, melt the butter with the flour in a medium pan and gradually whisk in the chicken stock. Boil for a minute, till thick and smooth, then remove from the heat. Whisk the egg yolk and cream in a heatproof jug, then gradually whisk in 3 tablespoons of the hot sauce, before adding this back into the pan. Bring to a simmer for 1 minute, stirring constantly, then add the lemon juice and generous seasoning to taste. This jiggerypokery will result in the most beautiful savoury sauce you ever did taste.

5 To assemble, choose a shallow, ovenproof dish that will comfortably hold the rolled crêpes and spread the bottom and sides with 2 tablespoons of

FOR THE CRÊPES
1 egg, any size
130 ml/4½ fl oz./generous ½ cup milk
3 tbsp water
80 g/3 oz./⅔ cup minus 1 tbsp flour
¼ tsp salt
15 g/1 tbsp butter, melted, plus extra for frying

FOR THE DUXELLES
250 g/9 oz. flat mushrooms
20 g/1½ tbsp butter
1 small shallot, finely chopped
a little finely chopped fresh parsley and snipped chives

FOR THE VELOUTÉ SAUCE
25 g/2 tbsp butter
20 g/2⅓ tbsp flour
200 ml/6¾ fl oz./¾ cup chicken stock, preferably home-made
1 egg yolk, any size
75 ml/2½ fl oz./⅓ cup double/heavy cream
a squeeze of lemon juice

FOR THE FILLING
90 g/3¼ oz./¾ cup chopped ham
a little finely chopped fresh parsley or tarragon
a squeeze of lemon juice
40 g/1½ oz./scant ½ cup grated Gruyère
a sprinkling of panko crumbs
a little extra butter

TRICK OF THE TRADE

*If you have to buy rather than grow your **fresh herbs**, you always end up with too much for one meal. I rinse or soak herbs carefully (if you doubt me, see what's in the water after you've washed them), then spin them dry in a small salad spinner. Chives (bundled with a rubber band), tarragon and basil are lightly enfolded in kitchen paper towels and put in a food bag in the fridge. Parsley, thyme and rosemary are chopped and left uncovered in the fridge, to 'air-dry' for up to 3 days. Fresh bay leaves live in the freezer. As for dill – see Trick of the Trade on page 28.*

the sauce. Mix the duxelles with the ham, parsley and 4 tablespoons of the sauce in a medium bowl, adding a little more sauce if necessary so the mixture sticks together. Add the lemon juice and taste for seasoning. Put ⅙ of the sauce on the bottom half of a crêpe and roll it up (don't tuck in the ends). Repeat with remaining crêpes and arrange in the dish. Mask the crêpes with the remaining sauce, then the cheese, before finally dotting with a few crumbs and tiny bits of butter. Bake at 170°C fan/190°C/375°F for about 30 minutes, till bubbling and lightly browned. If you enjoy a crunchy topping, preheat the grill/broiler to high, and grill for 1 minute at the end. Leave to cool for 5–10 minutes before serving.

TRICK OF THE TRADE

I am grateful to my fellow podcaster Rosie Birkett for her brilliant formula for **chicken crackling**, *which raises humble chicken skin – which you might normally throw away – to glory. Pull the skins off the chicken breasts and spread them out on a sheet of baking parchment. Season one side with plenty of salt, pepper and a shake of paprika, then flip over and repeat. Transfer the parchment to a shallow, rimmed baking tin or pan, lay another sheet of parchment on top, then put another baking tin on top of that, to weigh the skin down. Roast at 180°C fan/200°C/400°F for 25–30 minutes until bronzed and brittle.*

Chicken with 20 cloves of garlic & crackling

This is an adaptation of a winning dish I made in my MasterChef quarter-final, all those years ago. Cooking garlic cloves slowly in the oven transforms them into what the French call perles (pearls), with a mellow, nutty flavour, the texture of haricot beans and a pearly translucence. If you are concerned you may reek of garlic after eating so much, scientific research suggests that crunching on an apple, lettuce, or leaves of fresh mint are effective antidotes.

I strongly recommend buying chicken breasts with skin, and transforming the skin into crisp, bacon-like crackling (see Trick of the Trade, left). The best foil for this sophisticated dish is rice, to soak up the golden sauce. I find the most elegant way to serve rice is in a timbale – see details on page 12.

1 Bake the garlic in advance. Put the garlic in a small pan, add water to cover and bring to the boil. Simmer for 3 minutes. Drain, then use a small knife to help you slip the garlic cloves out of their skins. Put them in a small, ovenproof dish, add the butter and sprinkle with sugar. Bake, uncovered, at 100°C fan/120°C/250°F for 2 hours, shaking the dish occasionally, until the garlic is soft when poked with a knife and palest gold. Set aside, covered, until dinnertime.

2 If you have time, freeze the chicken for 15 minutes, to make it easier to handle. Slice almost through the centre of 1 chicken breast and open it up like a book to make a heart-shaped escalope. Repeat with the other one. Wipe 1 escalope with a little oil, cover with plastic film and bash with a mallet or rolling pin until a more or less uniform 1 cm/³⁄₈ inch thick. Move carefully to a plate and repeat with the remaining escalope.

3 To cook, heat ½ the butter in a large frying pan until foaming, then add the escalopes and seasoning. Cook without moving for 2 minutes, until spotty brown underneath. Flip over for another 1–2 minutes, till just cooked through, then transfer to serving plates. Cover with foil and put in a low oven to keep warm, while you…

4 Make the sauce by adding the remaining butter to the pan and bringing it to a sizzle. Add the shallot and cook for 30 seconds, till fragrant, then pour in the stock, scraping up any tasty bits on the base of the pan, and simmer for 3–4 minutes, till reduced to about 3 tablespoons. Swirl in the garlic pearls and 2 tablespoons of cream, heat through for 1 minute and check the seasoning. Simmer for 2 minutes if you prefer a thicker sauce, or loosen with a little extra cream. Serve the chicken drizzled with the sauce and a crackling shard, if making, and sprinkled with parsley.

FOR THE GARLIC
20 garlic cloves (unpeeled)
a knob/pat of butter
½ tsp sugar

FOR THE CHICKEN
2 chicken breasts (about 175 g/ 6 oz. each), with skin, if you wish to make chicken crackling (see Trick of the Trade, page 110)
a little oil
25 g/2 tbsp butter
1 shallot, finely chopped
100 ml/3⅓ fl oz./⅓ cup plus 1 tbsp chicken stock, or a mixture of stock and white wine
2–3 tbsp double/heavy cream or crème fraîche
a small handful of chopped fresh parsley, to garnish

Ratatouille cannelloni

This is something of a 'fusion' dish, in which lasagne sheets are rolled around a Provençal filling, in the style of Italian cannelloni. It can be made in advance to the end of step 4.

If you can only buy a large aubergine/eggplant, you will find a recipe for Pork & Aubergine Stir-fry on page 35, which will make good use of the remaining half.

FOR THE RATATOUILLE
2–3 tbsp olive oil, plus extra for
the dish
1 small, or ½ a large aubergine/
eggplant (200–250 g/7–9 oz.),
unpeeled, cut into 2-cm/
¾-in. chunks
1 small onion, chopped
1 small courgette/zucchini
(about 120 g/4¼ oz.),
cut into 2-cm/¾-in. chunks
1 garlic clove, crushed
3 medium tomatoes, halved,
deseeded and chopped
a large fresh rosemary sprig,
or ½ tsp dried oregano
2 bay leaves
100 ml/3⅓ fl oz./⅓ cup plus
1 tbsp stock, wine or water
8–10 pitted black olives, halved

FOR THE CHEESE SAUCE
25 g/2 tbsp butter
25 g/1 oz./3 tbsp flour
250 ml/8½ fl oz./1 cup plus
1 tbsp milk
100 g/3½ oz./1 cup grated
mature/sharp Cheddar,
or other strong cheese

FOR THE CANNELLONI
6 fresh or oven-ready (no-boil)
dried lasagne sheets
100 g/3½ oz. firm mozzarella,
sliced, or a 125-g/4½-oz.
buffalo mozzarella ball,
drained and sliced
2 tbsp grated Parmesan

1 For the ratatouille, heat 2 tablespoons of oil in a large frying pan till shimmering and add the aubergine. Season well and fry for 5 minutes. Add a little more oil, if necessary, the onion and courgette and fry for another 5 minutes, till the courgette is softening. Add the garlic and sizzle for 1 minute, then add the tomatoes, herbs and stock. Simmer for 10 minutes, until the vegetables are tender and the mixture well thickened. Discard the rosemary skeleton and bay leaves, stir in the olives, season well and set aside.

2 To make the sauce, put the first 3 ingredients in a pan and bring to a simmer, whisking constantly, to form a very thick white sauce. Simmer for 1 minute, then off the heat stir in the cheese. Season well.

3 If using dried lasagne sheets, fill a bowl with boiling water. Put in 3 sheets at a time and move them about to stop them sticking. After 3–4 minutes, fish them out with tongs or a fork and put on a board (do not stack them). Repeat with the remaining sheets. (This step is not necessary if using fresh lasagne sheets.)

4 Choose a shallow, ovenproof dish that will fit 6 rolled-up lasagne sheets (about 750-ml/3¼-cup capacity). Spread about ⅓ of the sauce over the base of the dish. To assemble the cannelloni, cover the bottom ⅔ of each sheet with ratatouille, then roll up from the bottom. Place, seam-side down, in the dish and continue with the remaining sheets. Tuck the mozzarella in between the cannelloni. Spoon the remaining sauce over the top and sprinkle with the Parmesan. (This dish can be made ahead up to this point and refrigerated for 24 hours, covered.)

5 Cover with foil and bake at 170°C fan/190°C/375°F for 25 minutes, then remove the foil and bake for 10–15 minutes longer, till lightly browned. Remove from the oven and allow to cool for 10 minutes before serving.

Sea bass fingers with tartar de luxe

An elegant version of the childhood favourite, which can be made with any skinless, boneless fish fillets of your choice. If your gherkins are the type that come in a jar with tiny cocktail onions, slice a couple into the sauce to add a little extra zing.

1 Ask your fishmonger to skin the fillets, or do it yourself by holding the fillet at one end on a board, skin-side down, then wiggling your knife underneath with the blade almost flat to the board. Trim any ragged bits off the fillets (if you have a cat, such scraps will be much appreciated) and slice each in half down the middle to make a total of 4 or 6 fingers.

2 Make yourself a production line of flour, egg and panko crumbs (see Trick of the Trade), with a spoon in each to help you as you go along. Season the flour and egg. Dip the first piece of fish in the flour, pressing it on well, then dunk in the egg and spoon it all over to cover. Lift it out, letting the excess egg drip off, and roll in the crumbs till completely covered. Press the crumbs on firmly and transfer to a plate. Continue with the remaining fillets. Sprinkle over any remaining crumbs.

3 *To make the tartar de luxe*, hard-boil/-cook the egg and cool. Mix the remaining ingredients, then peel and roughly chop the egg and fold in lightly. Check the seasoning and transfer to a small dish and refrigerate.

4 When ready to eat, heat the oil in a large frying pan till shimmering, lift out the fish fingers, shaking off the excess crumbs, and add to the pan. Cook for 2–2½ minutes, swirling the fillets around the pan so they cook evenly, then flip and cook for another 1–2 minutes. Serve at once with the tartar sauce, garnished with a few snipped chives, and lemon wedges.

FOR THE SEA BASS FINGERS
2 sea bass fillets, or other sustainable white fish (total weight 200–250 g/7–9 oz.)
2 tbsp flour
1 egg, any size, beaten
about 30 g/1 oz. panko crumbs (3 small handfuls)
2 tbsp oil
2 lemon wedges, to serve

FOR THE TARTAR DE LUXE
1 egg, any size
3 tbsp mayonnaise
finely grated zest and juice of ¼ a lemon
2 gherkins or cornichons, sliced
1 tsp wholegrain mustard
1 tsp creamed horseradish
1 tsp capers, rinsed if salted, roughly chopped
a handful of fresh chives or parsley, chopped, plus extra chives, snipped, to garnish
a splash of Tabasco

TRICK OF THE TRADE

Egg-and-breadcrumbing (known as 'pané-ing' in the business) gives a glorious crunchy finish to fish and meat, and is a technique which is a pain in the neck for big numbers, but practical for two.

Set yourself up with what you need before embarking on your recipe: a shallow dish for the flour, another for the egg, another for the crumbs, plus a plate on which to put the crumbed fish or meat. I have a set of rectangular interlocking metal dishes, bought for the purpose in the United States many years ago, which make the whole operation a pleasure.

I don't like waste, so I try and use the minimum of flour and crumbs (there's nothing you can do about the egg, and I usually end up throwing some away). It's annoying to run out halfway through, so keep the flour and crumbs to hand, in case you need to top up.

Poulet Vallee d'Auge

This classic from Normandy is the quintessential 'treat for two' – the sort of dish that would be impractical to serve to guests, and a bit too special for family eating. With its touch of drama (cue flames) it would make the perfect main course/entrée for a romantic supper.

I like to serve rice with this, as a foil for the creamy sauce (see page 12 for my timbale method), plus green beans or a vegetable of the season.

40 g/3 tbsp butter

2 small eating apples, peeled, cored and each sliced into 8 crescents

1 shallot, sliced

2 boneless chicken breast fillets, preferably skin-on (each about 200 g/7 oz.)

4 tbsp brandy or calvados

100 ml/3⅓ fl oz./⅓ cup plus 1 tbsp chicken stock, preferably home-made

100 ml/3⅓ fl oz./⅓ cup plus 1 tbsp crème fraîche or double/heavy cream

a squeeze of lemon juice

finely chopped fresh parsley, to finish (see Trick of the Trade)

1 Put ½ the butter in a large frying pan (one with a lid), heat until foaming then tip in the apples. Season and fry over a medium-high heat for 7–10 minutes, uncovered, turning constantly, until pale gold and completely tender (check by poking with a small knife – apples vary, so continue cooking if not). Remove with a slotted spoon and set aside.

2 Heat the rest of the butter in the pan and fry the shallot over a medium heat for 2–3 minutes, then push to the edge of the pan to prevent scorching. Add the chicken breasts, skin-side down, and cook without moving for 3 minutes (to encourage a tasty golden crust), then repeat on the other side.

3 Now the exciting bit. Heat ½ the brandy in a ladle or small pan. Remove from the heat and set light to it with a match or lighter, then judiciously pour it over the chicken in the pan and shake gently until the flames die down. Repeat with the remaining brandy.

4 Pour in the stock and simmer gently, covered, for 7–12 minutes, until the chicken is cooked and tender, then lift the chicken onto a carving board and leave to rest, covered with a piece of foil.

5 Return the apples and any juices to the pan and bubble the mixture vigorously to reduce to 3–4 tablespoons, then stir in the crème fraîche and lemon juice, season to taste and bring to a gentle simmer.

6 Meanwhile, carve each breast into 4–5 thick slices and add back to the pan to coat with the sauce. Serve sprinkled with parsley.

TRICK OF THE TRADE

Parsley *can be a divisive subject. I know that some cooks find it a pointless, unimaginative garnish, and complain that it tastes metallic, or of nothing at all. I disagree – chopped finely and evenly it has an appealing fresh, grassy flavour, its vibrant green colour makes almost any plate of food look more appetizing. Sticking my neck out still further, I find curly parsley tastes no different from flat-leaf, so being quicker and easier to chop, that's the one for me. I like to chop mine ultra-fine, which my friend Sam calls 'powdered parsley'.*

Mediterranean lamb with feta

Lamb neck fillet is my favourite cut for stews and casseroles – tender, juicy, no waste. Slice each fillet down the length, then into 3-cm/1¼-inch chunks. If your supermarket insists on selling you a 500-g/18-oz. pack, slice the lot and freeze half, ready for next time. (You can cook it from frozen by adding 10 minutes to the roasting time in step 1.) Diced leg and shoulder also work well. Lamb varies, so check the meat is completely tender before adding the pasta.

Casarecce is a short, twisted pasta shape from Sicily. Tagliatelle is a good alternative, but break the nests up before stirring them into the lamb. The anchovies are in the recipe to brighten the flavour – if you don't have any (perhaps because you hate anchovies), add a shake of Worcestershire sauce, or simply omit.

Before British novelist Fay Weldon wrote fiction, she was an advertising copywriter, and her favourite slogan was Vodka Gets You Drunker Quicker. In the case of this recipe, you can sprinkle the finished dish with chunks of any hard cheese, but You Can't Better Feta. Accompany with a simple Greek salad of tomato, cucumber and red onion with an olive oil-based vinaigrette and a scattering of black olives.

1 Mix the first 7 ingredients in an ovenproof saucepan, roasting tin or pan or dish and season well. Roast, uncovered, at 160°C fan/180°C/350°F for 45 minutes, stirring at half time (see Trick of the Trade). Add the tomatoes and wine and bring to the boil.

2 Cover tightly with a lid or foil, turn the heat down to 150°C fan/170°C/340°F oven and cook on for 1¼ hours more, until the lamb is tender, stirring once or twice.

3 Check the seasoning, stir in the pasta and cook on for another 20 minutes, till the pasta is cooked. Depending on how effectively your lid or foil did its job, you may need to add a splash or two of boiling water to keep the mixture moist. Serve sprinkled generously with crumbled feta.

TRICK OF THE TRADE

*My friend Mary Cadogan introduced me to the idea of **oven-browning meat and onions** for a stew or casserole, instead of doing it on the hob/stovetop. It's a seriously useful shortcut – it frees you up while it's in the oven, and keeps everything in one pan. The only rules are – make sure the meat is in one layer (not crowded in the pan) and stir at half time.*

250-g/9-oz. lamb neck fillet, cut into 3-cm/1¼-in. chunks
1 small onion, sliced
1 garlic clove, roughly chopped
2 anchovy fillets, roughly chopped (optional)
½ a cinnamon stick
½ tsp dried oregano
a good splash of olive oil
400-g/14-oz. can chopped tomatoes
400 ml/14 fl oz./1⅔ cups red or white wine, or water (I use the empty tomato can as a measure, 1 canful)
150 g/5½ oz. dried pasta, such as casarecce or tagliatelle
about 50 g/1¾ oz./⅓ cup crumbled feta, to finish

Rump steak béarnaise with potato wedges

It might sound simple, but putting a perfect steak dinner onto the table is no mean feat. When there are just two of you, however, it enters the realms of possibility. For me, rump is the most flavourful cut, though it does vary, so if you get the chance, specify the middle of the rump. I cook steaks using a sous-vide (see page 9) as this method delivers perfect, tender, juicy pieces of meat every time. I put seasoned, vacuum-packed steaks in for 1½–2 hours at 55 °C/130 °F (for medium-rare), dry them well, rub with a smashed garlic clove and sear in a very hot pan with a little butter.

Making an egg liaison sauce such as béarnaise in a sensible quantity for two is challenging, and this is the only method that works reliably for me. It is also accommodating, in that you can keep it warm for an hour or two, or even make it in advance and warm in the microwave.

I serve this in the 'steakhouse' manner, with a halved tomato on the plate (seasoned, sprinkled with herbs and garlic and turned in the steak pan), plus a salad or buttered spinach.

FOR THE WEDGES
2 or 3 large or baking potatoes (total weight about 300 g/ 10½ oz., or according to appetite), preferably red (purely for appearance), scrubbed and cut into thin wedges
2 tbsp oil
flaky salt or smoked salt, to serve

FOR THE BÉARNAISE
50 g/3½ tbsp butter, softened
2 egg yolks, any size
50 ml/1²⁄₃ fl oz./3½ tbsp boiling water
1 tsp wine vinegar
a pinch of cayenne pepper
2 or 3 stems of fresh tarragon, leaves stripped and chopped

FOR THE STEAK
2 rump steaks (each about 200 g/7 oz.) or other steaks of your choice
1 garlic clove, smashed (optional)
oil, for frying

1 Toss the potatoes in a spacious roasting tin or pan with the oil and plenty of seasoning. Roast for 45 minutes to 1 hour at 180°C fan/200°C/400°F, until browned and tender, shaking the pan every 10 minutes. Sprinkle with flaky salt or smoked salt before serving.

2 To make the béarnaise, set yourself up with a small pan containing a depth of about 1 cm/³⁄₈ inch of simmering water, and a heatproof bowl that will sit above it, without touching the water. Boil a kettle, fill a small jug/pitcher with boiling water and put it beside the hob/stovetop. Put the softened butter and egg yolks in the bowl, then place over the simmering water. Whisk constantly until the mixture melts into a mayonnaise-type consistency (about 1 minute), then over the course of another 2 minutes, slowly drizzle in the boiling water, whisking constantly. Continue whisking, monitoring the simmering water occasionally, for 5 more minutes, towards the end of which you will observe the sauce starting to thicken slightly. (It will be lighter and fluffier than regular hollandaise.) Turn off the heat, stir in the vinegar, cayenne and tarragon, season to taste and cover with plastic film. Leave over the pan of hot water till ready, whisking occasionally.

3 If cooking the steaks by sous-vide, see recipe introduction. If cooking in a pan, dry the steaks, rub with garlic, if using, and season well. Heat the oil till just smoking and fry the steaks for 2–3 minutes on each side, to your desired doneness (if you use a digital thermometer, insert it through the side of the steak into the centre – 55°C/131°F for medium-rare). Rest the meat for 5 minutes. (Not necessary if cooking sous-vide) then serve the steaks draped with sauce plus wedges and other adornments.

TRICK OF THE TRADE

★ *Forgive me if you already know this, but when **peeling ginger** the easiest way is with a teaspoon. If you don't need it all at once, freeze the rest – and you can peel and chop from frozen.*

★ *It may sound like heresy, but my wok took up too much space and I long ago gave it to charity: I find a large **non-stick** frying pan/skillet does the job just as well. Some cooks buy inexpensive non-stick and replace them yearly, but I have now invested in expensive non-stick pans with a lifetime guarantee, and I love them.*

★ *When it comes to Chinese-inspired meals, I wouldn't, however, be without **tongs** – a handy size (27 cm/10¾ inches) is best.*

Sizzling pork with seaweed & crunchy noodles

If seaweed isn't your thing, never fear – this super-tasty garnish is nothing other than shredded greens frizzled in oil and tossed in seasoning. You can make it with bok choi or other greens, but be sure to discard as much stalk as possible, and shred it superfine. It's fun to make (put your extractor fan on as it is quite pungent) and uses the same pan as the crunchy noodles.

Traditionally, stir-fries use a modest amount of meat, but if you prefer more, the option is there. If using dried noodles, cook according to pack instructions (do not overcook), drain completely, remove a handful for frying, and keep the rest warm to add in at the end. Linguine, vermicelli or even spaghetti can be used if that's all you have.

1 Grate the shallot, garlic and ginger into a small bowl, or chop finely if you prefer, and add the chilli. In a jug/pitcher, mix the stock, peanut butter, rice wine, soy and oyster sauces, sesame oil and vinegar. Thinly slice the spring onions on the diagonal and put in a small bowl. Set aside while you make the crunchy noodles and seaweed.

2 *To make the crunchy noodles*, take a small handful of fresh or cooked dried noodles – about 35 g/1¼ oz. – and roll them about on kitchen paper towels to ensure they're completely dry. Put in a bowl, sprinkle with cornflour and toss to coat. Heat about 1 cm/⅜ inch of oil in a medium saucepan till shimmering (if you have a digital thermometer 180°C/356°F) and using tongs, drop the noodles into the oil. Move the noodles around until they twist, crisp and turn a pale toasty colour (2 minutes), then lift out (leaving the oil in the pan) onto fresh, paper towels. Season lightly and set aside, uncovered.

3 *To make the seaweed*, wash the leaves, discard the ribs and stems and dry thoroughly – easiest done in a salad spinner. (When you think the leaves are dry, spin them with a couple of pieces of kitchen paper towel to finish the job.) Stack the leaves and cut into shreds. Heat the oil again and fry the greens in 2 batches until they darken and begin to look like seaweed (about 2 minutes), then lift onto paper towels with a slotted spoon. Toss with the salt, sugar and five-spice and keep warm, uncovered.

4 Heat 1 tablespoon of the oil (it will be greeny-brown – discard the rest) in a large frying pan or wok and fry the pork till nicely browned (about 4 minutes). Stir in the shallot mixture and cook for 1–2 minutes, till fragrant, then pour in the stock mixture and bring to a simmer for about 2 minutes, till glossy and slightly thickened.

5 Stir in the remaining noodles and heat through (about 2 minutes), then put into bowls. Top with the spring onions, crunchy noodles and seaweed.

FOR THE PORK
1 shallot
3 garlic cloves
3-cm/1¼-in. piece of fresh ginger, peeled (see Trick of the Trade, page 122)
1 small fresh red chilli/chile, deseeded and finely chopped
200 ml/6¾ fl oz./¾ cup chicken stock
2 tbsp smooth peanut butter or tahini
2 tbsp Shaoxing rice wine or dry sherry
1 tbsp soy sauce
1 tbsp oyster sauce
2 tsp toasted sesame oil
1 tsp Chinese vinegar or wine vinegar
2 spring onions/scallions
125–250 g/4½–9 oz. pork sausage meat or minced/ ground pork or pork sausages, skins removed

FOR THE CRUNCHY NOODLES
250 g/9 oz. fresh egg noodles or 175 g/6 oz. dried noodles, cooked
2 tsp cornflour/cornstarch
oil, for frying

FOR THE SEAWEED
3–4 cabbage or kale leaves
½ tsp each of salt and sugar
a sprinkle of five-spice powder

Tsar-in-the-hole

If the name of this recipe puzzles you, it is a riff on the old-fashioned British comfort dish 'toad-in-the-hole'. Like many old place and pub names, the origins of toad-in-the-hole are lost in obscurity, but the basis of the dish is Yorkshire pudding, a tasty golden 'popover' normally served with roast beef and gravy for Sunday lunch.

Toad-in-the-hole includes sausages, but in my version, the pudding is filled with a simple beef stroganoff (hence the 'tsar') and topped with soured cream and snipped chives. For individual puds, you will need two small non-stick baking tins or pans, about 12 x 18 cm/4¾ x 7 inches. Alternatively, make a larger pud and divide it in two. This is the perfect meal for a cold winter evening – and, whenever you need it, the definitive formula for a crisp, airy Yorkshire pudding.

FOR THE YORKSHIRE PUDDINGS

2 eggs, any size
80 g/2¾ oz./⅔ cup minus 1 tbsp flour
100 ml/3⅓ fl oz./⅓ cup plus 1 tbsp milk, skimmed/skim milk, or milk with a splash of water added
1–2 tbsp oil, for baking

FOR THE BEEF STROGANOFF

1 rump steak (about 230 g/8 oz.)
1 tbsp oil
1 small onion, chopped
2 portabella mushrooms (about 200 g/7 oz. total weight), sliced 1 cm/⅜ in. thick
1 tsp flour
1 medium tomato, halved, deseeded and chopped
100 ml/3⅓ fl oz./⅓ cup plus 1 tbsp stock
1 tbsp brandy or dry sherry
90 ml/3 fl oz./⅓ cup soured cream
snipped chives or chopped fresh parsley, to garnish

1 First make the batter: for the airiest result, do this the day before, refrigerate and bring back to room temperature before using. If this doesn't fit in with your plans, don't worry. Whisk the all the ingredients (not the oil), plus a pinch of salt, together in a bowl till smooth (about 1½ minutes) and set aside. Pour the oil into each baking tin or pan so the base is just covered (don't be mean about this). Ten minutes before baking, put the baking tins into the oven at 210°C fan/230°C/450°F.

2 Dry the steak with a kitchen paper towel and season well. Heat the oil in a large frying pan, till just smoking, add the steak and cook for 2–3 minutes per side, until done to your liking. If you have a digital thermometer, insert it through the side into the centre of the steak – medium-rare will read about 55°C/131°F. Remove the steak to a plate, cover with a piece of foil and set aside (not in the oven). Fry the onion and mushrooms in the same pan with seasoning, for 7 minutes, till golden. Stir in the flour and cook for 1 minute, then add the tomato, stock and brandy. Simmer till smooth and slightly thickened (3–4 minutes) and set aside, covered. Just before serving, discard the fat from the steak, slice into thick matchsticks and stir into the sauce along with any steak juices and ½ the soured cream. Bring back to a simmer.

3 About 10–15 minutes before eating, divide the batter between the hot tins (see step 1) and bake for 10–15 minutes, till the batter has risen into a crisp, golden shell. Slide onto hot plates, fill with the stroganoff, dollop on the remaining soured cream and finish with chives or parsley.

LAZY
SUNDAYS

Sunday has its own special, unhurried atmosphere.
Take your time over these sumptuous recipes for two,
rich in flavour and worth every minute spent on them.

Spinach & leek spanakopita with smoky tzatziki

There is something magical about working with filo/phyllo pastry, and the snap and crackle as it emerges from the oven in golden glory. (See Trick of the Trade, page 130.) This traditional pie, which is one of the splendours of Greek cuisine, can equally well be made with frozen leaf spinach (drained and squeezed in the same way as fresh). I like to complete this meal with a bowl of smoky tzatziki, and a simple Greek-style salad of tomatoes, cucumber, red onion and black olives.

FOR THE SPANAKOPITA

250 g/9 oz./5 scant cups fresh
    leaf spinach, destemmed
1 tbsp oil
1 tbsp butter
1 leek, trimmed and thinly
    sliced
2 garlic cloves, crushed
75 g/2¾ oz./½ cup crumbled
    feta
3 tbsp grated Parmesan
3 tbsp Greek yogurt
finely grated zest and juice
    of ½ a lemon
plenty of freshly grated nutmeg
a pinch of cayenne pepper
a small bunch each of fresh
    mint and dill, finely chopped
1 egg, any size, beaten

TO ASSEMBLE

50 g/3½ tbsp butter, melted
about 150 g/5½ oz. filo/phyllo
    pastry sheets (see Trick of
    the Trade, page 130)
3 tbsp grated Parmesan
a sprinkling of sesame and
    nigella seeds

FOR THE SMOKY TZATZIKI

1 small cucumber
5 tbsp Greek yogurt
½ tsp crushed garlic
1 drop of liquid smoke (see
    Trick of the Trade, page 130)
a drizzle of extra virgin olive oil,
    to serve
a few pinches each of smoked
    flaky salt and ground sumac

1 Put the spinach in a large pan and sprinkle with salt. If you have just washed it, it will be wet – otherwise, add a splash of water. Raise the heat and cook, stirring, as the spinach wilts and reduces in volume. Transfer to a colander (no need to wash the pan) and leave to cool while you…

2 Heat the oil and butter in the same pan and add the leek and a pinch of salt. Cook over a medium heat till soft – about 8 minutes. Add the garlic and cook for 1 minute. Turn off the heat but leave in the pan.

3 Press the spinach down in the colander with a wooden spoon to remove as much water as possible, then go in with your hands and squeeze energetically until it forms a tidy ball in the palm of your hand. Chop roughly on a board and stir into the leek mixture.

4 Add the feta, Parmesan, yogurt, lemon zest and juice, nutmeg, cayenne and ½ the herbs to the spinach mixture (reserving the rest for the tzatziki) and stir until thoroughly mixed. Taste and season well – do not be timid – then mix in the egg.

5 Line a rimmed baking tray or sheet with baking parchment. Brush a rectangle approximately 25 x 12 cm/9¾ x 4¾ inches with melted butter in the centre of the parchment, to serve as a size guide for the pie.

6 Lay a sheet of filo on the rectangle and cut to size with scissors. Splash over a little melted butter and brush lightly. Repeat till you have 4 layers, buttering each time. Spoon the leek and spinach mixture evenly on top, leaving a narrow border around the edge. Now add a layer of filo as before, brush with butter and sprinkle with ¼ of the grated Parmesan. Try not to lose count as you repeat this 3 more times (4 layers in total). Finish with 2 more layers, brushed just with butter this time. Score the pie lightly in half and scatter with the seeds.

7 Bake at 180°C fan/200°C/400°F for about 20 minutes, till golden and crisp. Remove from the oven and leave to cool for 10 minutes.

8 *To make the smoky tzatziki,* halve the cucumber lengthwise and scrape out and discard the seeds of 1 half using a teaspoon. Take the deseeded half and coarsely grate about 10 cm/4 inches of it into a bowl (you can

use the remaining cucumber in a Greek salad, if making). Mix in the yogurt, the garlic and herbs and the liquid smoke and taste for seasoning. If the yogurt is very thick, you may need to add a splash of water to loosen to a saucy consistency. Refrigerate till ready to serve, and serve with a little extra virgin olive oil drizzled over, a sprinkle of smoked flaky salt and a dusting of sumac.

9 Cut the spanakopita in half and serve with the tzatziki and a Greek salad, if you wish.

TRICK OF THE TRADE

★ **Filo/phyllo pastry** dough comes in many shapes and sizes, and for this Spanakopita recipe I use about half a 300-g/10½-oz. pack. It is no problem at all if you end up with something of a patchwork of pastry – save the best sheets for the bottom (to give stability) and the top (because it looks better). We are advised to keep the pastry covered while working with it, to stop it drying out, but if you have everything to hand before assembly starts, I don't find this necessary.

★ You might be forgiven for thinking that **liquid smoke** is a synthetic flavouring, but it is made by distilling actual smoke from actual wood (often hickory). Used very sparingly, it's a neat shortcut when you want to add a woody, barbecue nuance to sauces, dressings and dips.

Beef short ribs braised in red wine with Parmesan polenta

This sumptuous dish is all cooked in one pan. If you braise the ribs a day ahead, cool the meat, vegetables and strained juices separately: discard the orange fat that sets at the top of the juices and resume the recipe at step 4. Because braising is a long process, and pans, lids and ovens never quite behave the same, keep an eye that there is enough liquid to keep the beef juicy, with plenty of steam when you lift the lid. Add more water or wine if necessary. (See Trick of the Trade on page 132 for an explanation of the cartouche used here and tips on deglazing.)

A nice finishing touch is roasted cherry tomatoes, on or off the vine. Put in a small roasting tin or pan, season, drizzle with oil, crush in a little garlic and put in the oven for the last 45 minutes.

1 Season the short ribs all over and put, bone-side down, in a medium ovenproof saucepan (one with a lid). Roast at 210°C fan/230°C/450°F for 45 minutes to 1 hour, uncovered, until the meat is well browned. Transfer the meat to a plate and – burn alert! – pour all but 1 tablespoon of the fat from the hot pan into a small dish and set aside. Transfer the pan to the hob/stovetop.

2 Fry the onion, carrot and celery, if using, in the fat, stirring often, for 3–4 minutes, till tinged with brown, then add the garlic for 1 minute. Now tip in the red wine, canned tomatoes, rosemary, bay leaves and seasoning and bring to the boil, scraping up any tasty brown bits from the bottom of the pan (known as deglazing). Nestle the beef into the liquid, bone-side up, cover with a cartouche and a lid, and braise at 130°C fan/150°C/300°F for 2½ hours, turning the beef occasionally, until the meat is completely tender, with not a hint of rubberiness.

3 Use tongs to lift the meat out and put on a plate. Discard the bones, if you wish. Strain the liquid into a separating jug (see page 148) or jug/pitcher. Transfer the drained vegetables from the sieve/strainer into a small bowl, discarding the bay leaves and rosemary skeleton. Keep the meat and vegetables warm in a low oven, covered in foil.

4 *To make the Parmesan polenta*, whisk the polenta, milk and seasoning in a small pan for 5 minutes, till thick and smooth. Stir in the butter and Parmesan, check the seasoning and keep warm. It will thicken as it waits, so whisk in extra milk or water to loosen as necessary.

5 Skim off the fat that has risen to the top of the meat juices and add to the small dish you started in step 1. You should be left with about 150 ml/5 fl oz./⅔ cup of sauce. Add a splash of extra wine if you wish, or to thicken, mix the flour to a paste with 2 teaspoons of the beef fat with

FOR THE SHORT RIBS
- 2 meaty beef short ribs (each about 300 g/10½ oz.)
- 1 onion, cut into 6 segments
- 1 small carrot, cut into 3-cm/1¼-in. chunks
- 1 celery stick/stalk, cut into 3-cm/1¼-in. chunks (optional)
- 2 garlic cloves, sliced
- ½ a 75-cl bottle of full-bodied red wine, plus a little extra if necessary
- 230-g/8-oz. can chopped tomatoes, or ½ a 400-g/14-oz. can
- 2 large fresh rosemary sprigs
- 2 bay leaves
- 2 tsp flour (optional)
- a squeeze of lemon juice
- 1 tbsp brandy

FOR THE PARMESAN POLENTA
- 35 g/1¼ oz./¼ cup polenta
- 200 ml/6¾ fl oz./¾ cup milk, plus extra if necessary
- 15 g/1 tbsp butter
- 4 tbsp grated Parmesan

a fork, and flick half into the bubbling sauce, whisking all the time. It will thicken and add gloss to the sauce. If you would like the sauce thicker, repeat. (Save any remaining beef fat for frying and roasting.) Check for seasoning and add lemon juice to brighten the flavour and brandy for extra richness and depth.

6 Serve the ribs on a bed of polenta with the vegetables, and sauce drizzled over all.

TRICK OF THE TRADE

★ *A **cartouche** sounds cheffy but works brilliantly. Cut a square of baking parchment big enough to cover the pan, scrunch it up tightly, unscrunch it and tear a hole in the middle the size of a large coin. Place this flat on the surface of the braise, to keep everything moist and ensure bits protruding from the liquid do not get tough, chewy or burnt. A neat alternative, if you have one handy, is a paper butter wrapper or wrappers.*

★ *After browning meat and veg, you often end up with crusty, slightly burnt bits on the bottom of the pan. Known as fond, these are super-tasty and will not make your dish taste burnt or bitter. They are best incorporated by adding wine or other alcohol, and scraping with a wooden spatula, the process known as **deglazing**.*

Black & white chicken

This lovely chicken dish was originated by one great British food writer, Jane Grigson, and taken a step further by another – her daughter Sophie. It was apparently a favourite in the Grigson household at Christmas, so if you find yourself with leftover turkey (or chicken), look no further. I like to serve it with saffron rice (see my timbale method on page 12) and green beans.

A great bonus of poaching chicken in this way is that you are left with a pot of chicken stock, to be used for a weeknight risotto, or frozen away in convenient quantities for sauces or gravy (see Trick of the Trade).

1 Put all the chicken ingredients in a medium pan (one with a lid), season with salt and cover with water. Bring to the boil – it will look unpromising at first – and simmer gently, covered, for 45 minutes, till the chicken thighs are tender and cooked through. (Although the addition of a lemon slice helps to prevent this, chicken cooked on the bone can retain a pinkish tinge – don't panic if this is the case.)

2 Lift the chicken into a colander and allow to drain over the stockpot. When cool enough to handle, transfer to a board, remove the skin and bones and put these back in the pan. (Strain the stock when convenient and use for another purpose.) Pull or cut the chicken flesh into strips. Put the whiter pieces in a bowl, and the darker, generally more tasty morsels, in a second bowl.

3 In a small pan, melt the butter and swirl in the cream. Heat gently, season well and add the lemon juice, which will thicken the sauce. Stir in the whiter chicken pieces and heat through.

4 Line a rimmed baking tray or sheet with foil. Whisk the black sauce ingredients until emulsified, stir in the darker chicken pieces and arrange in a single layer on the tray. Grill/broil till lightly browned and sizzling, about 5 minutes.

5 Make a mound of rice (see recipe introduction), surround it with the black and white chicken, scatter with chopped parsley and serve.

FOR THE CHICKEN
4 chicken thighs, with skin and bones
1 onion, sliced
1 carrot, thinly sliced
1 celery stick/stalk, thinly sliced (optional)
1 garlic clove, smashed
1 bay leaf
12 black peppercorns
1 lemon slice
fresh parsley stems (reserve a few leaves to garnish)
mushroom trimmings (optional)

FOR THE WHITE SAUCE
25 g/2 tbsp butter
150 ml/5 fl oz./²⁄₃ cup double/ heavy cream
a squeeze of lemon juice

FOR THE BLACK SAUCE
2 tbsp oil
1 tbsp Dijon mustard
1 tbsp chutney of your choice, chopped up if chunky
1 tbsp Worcestershire sauce
¼ tsp cayenne pepper

TRICK OF THE TRADE

*There are plenty of times when a **stock** cube, powder or one of those little pots of concentrate will do, to add a savoury depth of flavour to dishes. The next step up are pouches or cans of stock, which are somewhat more subtle, but at a price. If you want a 'real' chicken flavour, however – particularly for gravy, risottos, or sauces in which stock is reduced down – it is impossible to beat home-made. You will find a handful of recipes in this book where I have indicated that, in my opinion, home-made stock makes a real difference. Books have been written about* how to make stock, but here is how I go about it. You might think you need to start with a whole chicken, but not so. I have a bag in the freezer marked 'For stock' into which go chicken bones and offcuts, as well as fresh parsley stems and mushroom trimmings. I also keep my eyes open for chicken carcasses at my local butcher, and assorted wings and drumsticks.

The only essentials are chicken, onion (or large shallots) and carrot. It is not worth buying celery specially, unless you have a use for the rest. A couple of bay leaves and a dozen black peppercorns add flavour and aroma, as do parsley stems, if you have them. I don't add other herbs because they are inclined to break up and make the stock spotty. If you are poaching chicken for a dish, add salt, otherwise not.

To keep things simple, I tip everything into a pan (frozen items do not need defrosting), add just enough water to cover, and bring to a simmer. I prefer to add the minimum of water, resulting in a more concentrated stock.

I cover the pot and leave it to simmer gently for 2 hours: I have an induction hob, which I set to turn off automatically. If I happen to be passing, I give it a stir.

After cooling, straining and removing fat (easiest when chilled) I bag the stock in convenient quantities, label and freeze. It is one of the delights of the metric system that 200 ml of stock weighs 200 g, etc, which makes it easier to defrost just the amount you need – specially if you label carefully. (It's nearly the same in ounces – 8 fl oz./1 cup stock weighs 8.4 oz.) To defrost, I put the bag upside down in a jug/pitcher and microwave on high till either melted or hot, as required.

Rib of beef with gochujang sprouts & best-ever roasties

A single rib of beef – sometimes sold (French makes it sound grander) as côte de boeuf – will provide a sumptuous Sunday lunch for two, with a couple of slices left over for steak sandwiches. The way I roast it is to season it thoroughly for a few hours, or even better, the night before, then roast at a low heat in the oven. Once the meat is medium-rare – and as usual, a digital thermometer comes in handy here – I transfer it to a very hot pan and sear it on all sides, to provide the browned crust that everyone loves so much. This technique is called reverse searing, with the advantage that the meat is almost entirely medium-rare, without a band of well-cooked and medium meat around the outside. (If you actually prefer it this way, sear the beef first, then roast at 200 °C fan/220 °C/450 °F for 12–15 minutes. Rest before serving.) Fans of the sous-vide can use that method. Vacuum-seal the meat in the usual way and sous-vide for 2–3 hours at 57 °C/134 °F, then sear as below.

This exciting roast merits an exciting side vegetable, so I suggest adorning Brussels sprouts with a savoury butter. If you haven't encountered gochujang, you are missing out: it is a sweet-sour-smoky chilli/chili paste from Korea, which lifts everything it touches, and I was inspired to try it by the clever chefs at Cooks' Illustrated. Marmite (yeast extract) makes a surprising, and tasty, alternative.

1 In advance, dry the beef with kitchen paper towels and season generously all over with flaky salt and freshly ground black pepper. Put on a rack set over a rimmed baking tray or sheet, and refrigerate uncovered. About 2 hours before cooking, remove from the fridge.

2 Put in a very low oven (still on the rack) at 100°C fan/120°C/250°F (yes, this is very low). Cook for about 1 hour until the centre of the meat is cooked to medium-rare: a digital thermometer inserted through the side of the roast into the centre should read 57°C/135°F (60–65°C/140–149°F for medium).

3 *For the gochujang sprouts*, fork together the butter with the gochujang and taste for seasoning. Halve the sprouts down the centre and fit as many as you can, flat-side down, in a large frying pan. Drizzle over the oil and heat till sizzling, then clap on the lid and cook until the underneath of the sprouts has started to brown – about 5 minutes. Remove the lid, move the sprouts about (without turning them over) and cook for a further 10–15 minutes till tender all the way through. Mix in the flavoured butter and serve hot.

4 As the beef comes out of the oven, heat the oil in a frying pan until beginning to smoke. Add the beef and butter and brown the meat quickly on all sides. Because the meat has been roasted so slowly, it does not need to be rested, so can be sliced and served immediately.

FOR THE RIB OF BEEF
a single rib of beef on the bone (700–900 g/1½–2 lb.)
1 tbsp oil
a generous knob/pat of butter

FOR THE GOCHUJANG SPROUTS
20 g/1½ tbsp butter
2 tsp gochujang paste, or ½ tsp Marmite (yeast extract)
150–200 g/5½–7 oz. Brussels sprouts, washed and trimmed
2 tbsp oil

FOR THE BEST-EVER ROASTIES (SEE METHOD ON PAGE 138)
2–3 medium potatoes, depending on appetite
2 tbsp oil
flaky salt, to finish

TRICK OF THE TRADE

*When it comes to **roasting potatoes**, most cooks have their favourite method. I learnt mine during a podcast I made with chef Tom Kerridge. (We are both mildly obsessed with potatoes.) It turns out that it's not a question of which potatoes you use, or fancy goose fat, but coating them with a sort of potato 'batter'. When boiling potatoes, always simmer gently, to prevent waterlogging, and use a delicate touch when turning the roasties, to preserve their tasty, lacy crust.*

1 For the best-ever roasties, peel the potatoes. Put the first one in front of you and cut off the bump at each end (do not discard), then slice the central, cylindrical section into 2-cm/¾-inch discs. Repeat with the remaining potato(es). Put the discs in a pan and add the offcut bumps, roughly chopped. Pour in water to cover, add salt, bring to the boil and simmer very gently, covered, for 7–10 minutes, till just tender. Use a slotted spoon to remove the discs to a colander to drain. Scoop the offcuts into a small bowl – they should be soft and crumbly – do not discard the cooking water. Mash the offcuts with a fork till smooth. Splash in 1–2 tablespoons of the cooking water and work till sticky, like wallpaper paste. Line a small rimmed baking tray or sheet with parchment paper and oil it liberally. Use a brush or small spatula to coat the top of the potato discs thickly with the paste (a messy operation, but this is how you create the delicious crust) and place, paste-side down, on the oiled paper. Smear more potato paste on top, then refrigerate, uncovered, until ready to cook. This can be done a day ahead.

2 To roast the potatoes, season them with salt and roast at 180°C fan/200°C/400°F for 35 minutes, till beginning to turn golden. Turn carefully – trying to keep the crust intact – and roast for 10–15 minutes more. When golden and crisp all over, they can be served, or kept hot. Serve sprinkled with flaky salt.

Slow roast pork belly with popcorn crackling & apple chutney

I am indebted to the cooks at America's Test Kitchen for finally – finally! – working out how to make perfect, super-crunchy pork crackling every time. The secret is to slow roast the pork, then fry it, fat-side down, in bubbling fat, so that it pops and crackles. Note that for this recipe the meat needs to be prepared and seasoned a day ahead of roasting.

This simple apple chutney is a sort of spicy apple sauce. It contains several variables – how the apple cooks down, the sweetness of the apple and cider – so I suggest you taste at the end and make any necessary adjustments.

1 Sharpen your knife and make diagonal cuts across the skin of the pork belly, about 1 cm/³/₈-inch apart, cutting through the skin to the fat below. These cuts will later serve as your guide for carving the pork. Now cut the pork belly in half lengthwise, to make 2 strips, each about 6 cm/2½ inches in width. Mix the flaky salt and sugar and rub all over the meat sides of the pork, then rub the table salt over the skin. Put the pork in a dish or bowl (to catch any juices) in the fridge, uncovered, for 24 hours.

2 Set a small rack over a roasting tray and grease the rack or spray with oil or non-stick spray. Put the pork on the rack (discard any juices) and roast at 110°C fan/130°C/265°F for 3–3½ hours. The meat should be very tender when poked with a knife and if you have a digital thermometer, it should read 90°C/194°F when inserted into the thickest part of the meat. Remove the pork to a plate, cover with foil and leave for up to 1 hour.

3 *For the apple chutney*, heat the oil in a medium saucepan and cook the shallot, apple and ginger gently, stirring often, till beginning to soften (it depends on the apples, but about 5 minutes). Stir in 2 teaspoons of sugar, the cider, spices and raisins (if using) and cook for 4–5 minutes longer, till the mixture is saucy and glistening. Season with salt and extra sugar if necessary and set aside, covered.

4 To crackle the skin of the pork, put the oil into a small frying pan and add the pork, skin-side down. Raise the heat and fry steadily for about 8 minutes, moving the pork occasionally, until the skin blisters ('popcorns') and turns golden and crisp. Leave to rest for 5–10 minutes, then sprinkle the crackling with a little salt and sugar to finish. Remove to a plate and carve (or cube) along the cuts you made previously, and serve with the warm apple chutney.

FOR THE PORK BELLY
- a 400–500-g/14–18-oz. piece of pork belly, with skin, no bones
- 2 tsp flaky salt
- 2 tsp sugar, plus a little extra to finish
- ¼ tsp table salt
- 100 ml/3⅓ fl oz./⅓ cup oil

FOR THE APPLE CHUTNEY
- a little oil, for frying
- 1 shallot, roughly chopped
- 1 small eating apple, peeled and cut into 1.5-cm/⅝-in. chunks
- 1-cm/³/₈-in. piece of fresh ginger, grated
- 2–3 tsp soft brown or caster/superfine sugar
- 100 ml/3⅓ fl oz./⅓ cup plus 1 tbsp cider (hard), or white wine
- a pinch of ground coriander, or ground cloves
- ½ tsp mustard seeds (optional)
- 2 tsp raisins or sultanas/golden raisins (optional)

Russian fish pie with soured cream sauce

This is coulibiac, the classic Russian dish of salmon, mushrooms and eggs encased in pastry. In the early 20th century, the great French chef Escoffier brought the recipe to Paris, and complicated it by the addition of pancakes (to keep the layers separate), brioche pastry and myriad other refinements. My version lets the ingredients speak for themselves, and most of the work is in actually assembling the dish.

If your fishmonger or supermarket sells 'fish pie mix', that can be used instead of straight salmon. This sophisticated dish needs only a simple accompaniment – what my friend Nellie would describe as a 'quiet vegetable'. Broccoli, or its aristocratic cousin Tenderstem, are good.

FOR THE PIE
30 g/1 oz./scant ¼ cup long
    grain or risotto rice
2 eggs, any size
40 g/3 tbsp butter, plus extra
    if you wish
1 small onion, chopped
100 g/3½ oz. chestnut
    mushrooms, trimmed
    and sliced
a 200-g/7-oz. salmon fillet,
    skinless, cut into 2.5-cm/
    1-in. cubes
finely grated zest of ¼ a lemon
a small handful of fresh dill
    leaves, chopped
a pinch of cayenne pepper
a pack of ready-rolled puff
    pastry dough (you will need
    about 320 g/11½ oz.)
2 tbsp soured cream

FOR THE SOURED CREAM SAUCE
finely grated zest of ¼ a lemon
5 tbsp soured cream
1 tbsp mayonnaise
½ tsp Dijon mustard
a pinch each of sugar and
    cayenne pepper
a little chopped fresh dill,
    plus extra to garnish
paprika, to dust

1 Cook the rice by bringing a small pan of salted water to the boil, adding the rice and simmering, covered, for 12–15 minutes till tender. Drain and leave the rice in the colander to cool. Hard-boil/-cook one of the eggs by putting into a pan of cold water to cover, bringing to a rolling boil, then turning off the heat and clapping on a lid plus a folded tea towel/dish cloth to keep the heat in. After 10 minutes, remove the egg, dent the shell and cool quickly under running water. This produces a perfectly cooked egg and a yolk without a hangover (dark circle). Shell and slice.

2 Heat 15 g/1 tablespoon of the butter in a medium frying pan and add the onion and seasoning. Fry for 4–5 minutes till golden, then add the mushrooms and cook for 2–3 minutes, till lightly browned but still juicy. Leave in the pan to cool. Mix the salmon with the zest, dill, cayenne and plenty of seasoning.

3 To assemble, unroll the pastry. Keep it on its paper, but sprinkle a little flour underneath. Lightly mark a 7 x 21-cm/2¾ x 8¼-inch rectangle in the centre, using a ruler and the handle of a teaspoon, to act as a guide (do not cut through the pastry). Trying to keep a neat shape, spread ½ the rice over the rectangle in a very thin layer, then ½ the onion mixture, then all the chopped egg. Season well. Arrange the salmon on top, and blob over the soured cream. Finish by layering the remaining mushroom mixture and remaining rice (gently pat to keep the shape) on top.

4 Now the fun bit – imagine you're wrapping a gift. Beat the remaining egg. First brush the exposed pastry with beaten egg. Bring each short end up and lay onto the top rice layer. Trim away some of the excess pastry on the side flaps, then bring up the sides and press firmly together on top. Use your hands to neaten and firm it up all around.

In the past I have urged cooks to use large eggs. Thanks to the British Hen Welfare Trust, I have recently changed my thinking. The fact is that small and medium eggs have numerous all-round advantages. For the hen, they are easier to lay. For farmers, being able to sell mixed-size eggs means not having to sell small ones for a pittance. And for consumers, smaller eggs are actually better as they contain more yolk, proportionately, than large and the white is less watery.

5 Line a rimmed baking tin or pan with baking parchment and invert the pie onto it. Peel away and discard the top paper. Mark the pie with a few shallow slashes (do not cut it, just drag over the tip of a knife), then make 2 holes in the top. Brush all over with beaten egg. (It can be refrigerated at this point for up to 1 hour.)

6 Just before baking, melt ½ the remaining 25 g/2 tablespoons butter and spoon as much as you can into the holes in the top. Brush any remaining melted butter, plus a little more if you wish, over the coulibiac. Bake at 200°C fan/220°C/450°F for 20–25 minutes, till golden and crisp. While it bakes, mix the ingredients for the soured cream sauce and put in a small bowl, then dust with paprika and dill. Leave the coulibiac to rest for 5–10 minutes, then cut into 4 thick off-centre, slices and serve with the sauce.

Lamb fillet roast in sumac with saffron dauphinois

This is a miniature version of roast lamb. If you haven't encountered lamb loin fillet – sometimes called (on account of its shape) a cannon of lamb – this is the most choice and tender lamb cut of all, and perfect for two people. Because there is no waste, a small fillet – even 220 g/8 oz. – serves two people handsomely, and it is quick and easy to cook. An alternative is a 6-cutlet rack of lamb (about 350 g/12 oz.), which can be roasted in exactly the same way.

When planning your cooking, you may wish to start with the potatoes. The cooking time depends on how thinly you slice them, so although it's only a small amount of potato, I set up my mandoline on its finest setting. Do be absolutely sure the potatoes are tender and completely cooked through – check in several places – as chewy potatoes always disappoint.

The optional savoury butter and leek garnish are the sort of tasty, dare I say 'restauranty', flourishes that are practical if there are just two of you, and you don't mind having something to do at the last minute.

1 Dry the lamb fillet and season all over. Heat a little oil in a small frying pan and put in the fillet, fat-side down at first, then turning, for 2 minutes in total. Remove to a small roasting tin or pan lined with foil (for easy clean-up) and dust all over with the sumac. The fillet is now ready to cook, or it can wait for 30 minutes. Roast at 180°C fan/200°C/400°F for 12–15 minutes. Check doneness by poking with a knife, or if you have a digital thermometer, it should read 54°C/129°F (for rare) or 60°C/140°F (medium). Fold the foil up around the meat loosely and leave to rest for 5–10 minutes before carving into slices and serving.

2 *To make the mint and sumac butter*, if using, mix all the ingredients with salt and pepper, spoon into a small pot or bowl and put in the fridge. Add a spoonful on each portion of lamb when serving.

3 *For the saffron dauphinois*, heat the butter in a small frying pan and add the onion and seasoning. Fry slowly and gently for 15 minutes, till golden and frizzled. Meanwhile, bring the cream, saffron and nutmeg just to the boil in a medium saucepan, then turn off the heat, season and cover. Slice the potatoes as thinly as you can (I recommend a mandoline) and add to the cream. Bring the mixture to a simmer, stirring constantly with a rubber spatula to stop the mixture sticking. Butter a shallow, ovenproof dish – about 19-cm/7½-inches square (top measurement), 300-ml/10-fl oz. (1¼-cup) capacity – and layer in ½ the potatoes, followed by all the onion and ½ the cheese. Add the remaining potatoes, top with the cheese and a few crumbs and bake at 160°C fan/180°C/350°F for 30–40 minutes. Check the potatoes are fully cooked and tender by poking with a knife in 3 or 4 different spots. Once done, set aside to cool slightly.

FOR THE LAMB
a 220–300-g/8–10½-oz. lamb loin fillet
a little oil, for frying
½ tsp ground sumac

FOR THE MINT & SUMAC BUTTER (OPTIONAL)
25 g/2 tbsp butter, softened
12 fresh mint leaves, chopped
¼ tsp ground sumac
a little crushed garlic

FOR THE SAFFRON DAUPHINOIS
15 g/1 tbsp butter, plus extra for the dish
1 small onion, thinly sliced
120 ml/4 fl oz./½ cup double/heavy cream
a large pinch of saffron threads
a grating of fresh nutmeg
250 g/9 oz. potatoes, peeled
40 g/1½ oz./⅓ cup grated Gruyère
a sprinkling of panko crumbs, or fresh breadcrumbs

FOR THE LEEK STRAW (OPTIONAL)
1 small leek, split, washed and dried
1 tbsp oil

4 To make the leek straw, if using, cut off a 4-cm/1½-inch section of leek, roughly where the white meets the green. Slice as thinly as you can into matchsticks. (If you wish, boil the remaining leek and serve as a side vegetable.) Shortly before serving, heat the oil in a small frying pan, add half the leek and cook until golden (the colour of straw). Remove immediately to a piece of kitchen paper towel and repeat with the remaining leek. Keep warm in the oven if necessary before sprinkling with salt and serving on top of the lamb and butter.

TRICK OF THE TRADE

Sumac and saffron are two spices that I could not live without. Ground sumac has a fine poppy seed-like texture and purply red colour. Think of it as lemon pepper, and use it generously – both in cooking and as a seasoning – to lift and brighten flavours. It has a particular affinity with lamb, and a light sprinkle brings out the flavour of feta cheese and hummus.

I first encountered sumac when experimenting with Persian cooking, and that is where my saffron comes from, too, thanks to my generous friend Farnaz Massoumian, who spends part of the year in Tehran. Saffron has a reputation for being colossally expensive – and so it should be, because the tiny filaments have to be picked by hand. Considering how little you use at a time, however – usually just a pinch – and its fragrance and impact, I cannot think of it as an extravagance.

Three-hour shoulder of lamb

There is an art to braising, and it results in the tenderest, most flavoursome meat you can imagine. In France, shoulders or legs of lamb are lingeringly braised for 7 hours, till they can be 'carved' with a spoon and fork, but for a half-shoulder or leg, 3 hours does it. This recipe employs the same basic techniques as the Beef Short Ribs on pages 131–132, where you will find insights into deglazing, how to make a cartouche, and how to remove fat from braising juices.

I like to serve this on a bed of canned flageolet beans, drained and reheated with a little butter and a crushed garlic clove folded through, plus the braising vegetables.

1 half-shoulder or half-leg
   of lamb on the bone
   (800–900 g/1¾–2 lb.)
a splash of oil
1 onion, cut into 6 segments
1 carrot, cut into 3-cm/
   1¼-in. chunks
1 celery stick/stalk, cut into
   3-cm/1¼-in. chunks
   (optional)
2 garlic cloves, sliced
½ a 75-cl bottle of full-bodied
   white or red wine, or water
2 large fresh rosemary sprigs
2 bay leaves
a small knob/pat of butter and
   2 tsp flour (optional)
1 tbsp brandy (optional)

TO SERVE (OPTIONAL)
400-g/14-oz. can flageolet
   beans, drained and rinsed
1 garlic clove, crushed (optional)
a knob/pat of butter

1 Dry the lamb and season all over. Heat the oil in a medium ovenproof saucepan (one with a lid) and fry the lamb on all sides over a high heat, until well browned – about 3–5 minutes. Transfer the meat to a plate.

2 Fry the onion, carrot, celery (if using) and garlic in the remaining fat, stirring often, for 3–4 minutes, till tinged with brown. Tip in the wine, rosemary, bay leaves and seasoning and bring to the boil, deglazing the pan. Nestle the lamb in the liquid, cover with a cartouche and lid, and oven-braise at 130°C fan/150°C/300°F for 3 hours, turning the lamb twice, until it is totally tender and falling away from the bone.

3 Use tongs to lift the meat out and put it on a plate. Strain the braising liquid into a separating jug (see Trick of the Trade) or regular jug/pitcher. Transfer the drained vegetables from the sieve/strainer into a small bowl, discarding the rosemary skeleton and bay leaves. Keep the meat and vegetables warm in a low oven, covered in foil.

4 Remove as much fat as you can from the surface of the braising liquid and transfer to a small saucepan. Bring to a simmer. If you wish to thicken the juices, mash the butter and flour to a paste and flick bits into the boiling juices, whisking all the time and adding only as much as needed to achieve the desired thickness. Taste for seasoning – add salt to soften and sweeten the wine flavour, brandy for depth and richness.

5 Arrange beds of reheated garlicky and buttered flageolet beans, if liked, and braising vegetables on plates. Use a spoon and fork to pull off hunks of lamb and place on top. Drizzle over the rich sauce.

TRICK OF THE TRADE

*If you enjoy braising, a **separating jug** is a useful piece of kit. I have one that you tilt, and the jug keeps back the fat. And another, more ingenious one by Oxo Good Grips®, with a little tap underneath, which allows you to drain the good stuff and hold back the fat. If you have time to chill the juices, so the fat can collect at the top and be spooned away, a normal jug/pitcher is your best choice.*

SWEET DREAMS

A sprinkling of desserts and bakes created expressly for the smaller household, to enjoy when you fancy something sweet but don't want to be eating it up for the rest of the week.

Strawberry & mascarpone tartlets

This exquisitely brittle, featherlight pastry needs a light touch, but once you have the knack you can top it with any fruit of the season.

1 Mix the flour and butter in a small food processor, or rub the butter in by hand. Add the sugar and keep mixing until the mixture comes together into a crumbly ball (do not add any liquid). Flatten into a thin disc with your hands, wrap in plastic film and chill in the fridge for 10–15 minutes, till firm.

2 Flour the disc lightly on both sides, place on the plastic film and lay another sheet of plastic film on top. Roll out very thinly and cut out 2 circles each 10 cm/4 inches in diameter, rerolling scraps if you need to. Use the thin metal base of a tart tin or pan or palette knife to transfer the pastry circles to a baking tray or sheet (no need to grease). Bake at 170°C fan/190°C/375°F for 11–13 minutes, rotating the tin at half time, till pale nut brown, fragrant and just firm to the touch. Remove from the oven and count to 10. Now slide a palette knife under the first pastry circle, and nudge it so it releases from the baking tray. Repeat with the second. Let the pastry cool on the tray, nudging occasionally to stop it sticking. When cool, move the tray to an undisturbed spot and cover with plastic film. These can be made a couple of hours ahead.

3 When the time comes, move the discs to flat serving plates using the tart tin base or a palette knife. Put the mascarpone, sugar and vanilla in a small bowl and beat with a wooden spoon, then use a fork or the back of a spoon to spread on the tart bases, right to the edges. Top with sliced strawberries, dust with a little extra icing sugar and serve.

30 g/1 oz./¼ cup self-raising/
   rising flour, or 30 g/1 oz./
   ¼ cup plain/all-purpose flour
   plus ¼ tsp baking powder
15 g/2 tbsp plain flour
35 g/2½ tbsp butter
2 tsp demerara/turbinado sugar

FOR THE TOPPING
3 tbsp mascarpone
   (see Trick of the Trade)
icing/confectioners' sugar,
   to taste
a few drops of vanilla extract
6–8 fresh strawberries, sliced
   or halved

TRICK OF THE TRADE

★ *When it comes to **manoeuvring pastry and cakes**, I find the thin metal base of a tart tin or pan (one with no rim) indispensable, because you can slide it under without damaging the fragile edge. A 'cake lifter' does the same job, but is one more thing to find a home for in your kitchen cupboard.*

★ ***Leftover mascarpone*** *induces – in me, at least – a sense of guilt, so if the rest of your tub is likely to be wasted, use double/heavy cream instead, whipped with the sugar and vanilla. I have been known – with a slight sense of failure – to consign leftover mascarpone to the freezer. The texture is never quite the same, but you can use it to luxe up mashed potato, or give a creamy finish to a risotto.*

Chocolate brandy crunch

I have always been drawn to recipes that don't require actual cooking, and in 2004 wrote a whole book about them (The No-Cook Cookbook). I felt rather outdone when in 2013 my friend Miriam Nice went one better and wrote Cooking Without a Kitchen, in which food is 'cooked' on radiators, and pancakes are made using a household iron. (If this is a genre which captures your imagination, I can also recommend Manifold Destiny, billed as 'The One! The Only! Guide to Cooking on your Car Engine'.)

This sophisticated and luxurious teatime or after-dinner treat is as simple as turning on the microwave. You will need a loaf tin or pan measuring about 20 x 10 cm/8 x 4 inches at the base, lined with baking parchment, foil or plastic film. (Fold the parchment over the upside-down tin to get the shape, then add a few dots of butter to the inside of the tin to help stick it in place.) If, like me, you are a fan of crystallized or stem ginger, add a little, finely chopped, to the dried fruit.

100 g/3½ oz./¾ cup dried fruit, sultanas/golden raisins, raisins, or a mixture

4 tbsp brandy, rum, sherry or fruit juice

150 g/5½ oz. dark/bittersweet chocolate, or a mixture of dark and milk/semisweet

50 g/3½ tbsp butter

1 tbsp golden syrup/light corn syrup or maple syrup

7 digestive biscuits/cookies, or 7 graham cracker sheets (about 100 g/3½ oz.)

50 g/1¾ oz./scant ½ cup roasted hazelnuts, chopped, or toasted flaked/slivered almonds

a little cocoa powder, for dusting (optional)

1 Put the dried fruit in a small bowl with the liquor and microwave for 45 seconds to 1 minute until steaming, then set aside.

2 Break up the chocolate (see Trick of the Trade) and put into a medium bowl with the butter and syrup. Microwave for 1–2 minutes till melted.

3 Break the biscuits or crackers into the chocolate, then use a spatula to fold in the fruit, brandy and nuts, so that everything is thoroughly chocolatized. Turn into the lined loaf tin or pan and leave to set for 3 hours, then put in the fridge for 4 hours, or overnight. (If you chill it immediately, it will lose its sheen.) Remove from the baking tin, peel away the parchment, lightly dust with cocoa powder (if using) and cut into squares or bars to serve.

TRICK OF THE TRADE

Chopping chocolate *is a job I try to avoid. If the chocolate is in bar form, I smash it on the work surface (still in its wrapper) then snap it (still wrapped in its paper, or foil) into a bowl. This rough and ready approach will require a little more care (and stirring) while melting, but saves getting covered in the stuff. When I see them, I buy good-quality chocolate chips, which have the added attraction that you can stir a handful into your breakfast cereal if you want to start the day with a swing.*

Anything crumble

Apple crumble is one of the mellow treats of autumn/fall, but why stop there? In my restaurant days, I discovered that instead of piling everything into a dish and hoping for the best, you could get consistently luscious fruit and crumbly crumble by cooking the components separately. This recipe makes enough crumble topping for 2–4 individual crumbles, depending on your appetite.

1 The crumble can be made in advance and kept in a plastic box in the fridge for up to 2 weeks. Put the first 6 ingredients in a small food processor and whizz to mix, then add the vanilla and almond extracts, butter and ½ the nuts and process again to crumbs. Finally, pulse in the remaining almonds, so they don't get chopped too much. Line a rimmed baking tray or sheet with a piece of baking parchment and tip in the crumble mixture. Level and pat it reasonably firm using a spatula (which will ensure it forms clumps, rather than powder) and bake at 160°C fan/180°C/350°F for 10–15 minutes, till lightly browned and firm.

2 This is a good recipe for control freaks, as you make all the decisions. Prepare your fruit (peel, core, remove stones, as appropriate) and slice or cut into chunks. Mix some sugar with spice if using, and cornflour if your fruit is very juicy (for instance pears, peaches, rhubarb). Add a squeeze of lemon juice, if liked. Cook gently together in a pan with sugar to taste till tender – you'll find my flavour suggestions in Trick of the Trade (below).

3 To bake, put the fruit in individual baking dishes or gratin dishes and top with the crumble – pat it lightly into shape with the back of a spoon. Sprinkle with the demerara and bake at 170°C fan/190°C/375°F for 12–15 minutes, till the fruit is bubbling. Allow to cool for 10 minutes before serving with cream or any of the other suggestions given.

TRICK OF THE TRADE

*If you like to experiment, there are excellent books on **flavour pairing**, which encourage one to extend one's gustatory horizons. When it comes to crumble, I like the following combinations, according to mood and what's in season. If you have any favourites I've missed, I'd love to know them. Plus, I almost always add a squeeze of lemon juice.*

apple + ground cinnamon, ground coriander + orange zest + raspberries or mincemeat (macerated and spiced chopped dried fruit)
pear + ground ginger + calvados (apple brandy)
rhubarb + strawberries + vanilla extract
peach or nectarine + blueberries or cherries or raspberries + vanilla + brandy
plum + ground cinnamon + Amaretto (almond liqueur)

FOR THE CRUMBLE
70 g/2½ oz./½ cup plus
   ½ tbsp flour
25 g/2 tbsp white sugar
25 g/2 tbsp soft brown sugar
¼ tsp ground cinnamon
a little freshly grated nutmeg
¼ tsp salt
1 tsp vanilla extract
a few drops of almond extract
45 g/3 tbsp butter
35 g/1¼ oz./⅓ cup flaked/
   slivered almonds, toasted
   if liked

FOR THE FRUIT
2 eating apples or pears,
   or a mixture of fresh fruit
   of your choice
a squeeze of lemon juice
   (optional)
sugar, flavourings and spice to
   taste (see Trick of the Trade)
1 tsp demerara/turbinado sugar
½ tsp cornflour/cornstarch
   (only if your fruit is very juicy)
double/heavy cream, whipped
   cream, clotted cream,
   custard/custard sauce or
   ice cream, to serve

Mandarin trifle

Trifle is one of those desserts that smaller households miss out on – most recipes seem to be devised on the Downton Abbey scale, to serve huge family gatherings. It is seriously quick and simple to make for two – the custard cooks in a flash, and the cream whips up in under 1 minute (no need to get out the electric beaters for such a small quantity).

Serve this in a shallow dish of about 750-ml/3¼-cup capacity – glass is ideal, so you can enjoy the layered effect. If you choose 2 individual glasses, as shown, go for wide rather than deep, so you don't have to dig down too far for the liquory goodness.

A nice finishing twist – if you are using marmalade – is to remove half a dozen shreds of peel from the jar, and place them on the cream as a zesty candied topping. The alternative, more traditional, is a sprinkle of toasted almonds – add these just before eating, so they don't go soft.

150 ml/5 fl oz./⅔ cup double/
  heavy cream
2 tbsp milk
1 egg yolk, any size
2 tsp sugar
½ tsp cornflour/cornstarch
¼ tsp vanilla extract
½–1 orange or lemon muffin
  (depending on appetite)
1 tbsp orange marmalade
  or apricot jam/preserve,
  plus a few shreds from
  the jar if using marmalade
2 tbsp orange liqueur,
  Amaretto or brandy
2 mandarins, clementines,
  satsumas or tangerines,
  plus juice of 1 extra
a 120-g pot ready-made orange
  jelly, or 4 oz. of Jell-o orange
  gelatin dessert (about
  1½ servings) (in the US)

1 Make the custard first, by bringing ⅔ of the cream and the milk to the boil in a small pan. While it is heating, whisk the egg yolk, sugar, cornflour and vanilla in a heatproof bowl or jug/pitcher. Pour the hot cream over the yolk mixture, whisking all the time, then pour the mixture back into the pan. Bring to a simmer, still whisking, at which point it will thicken. Remove from the heat and leave to cool (a metal bowl will speed this up) while you assemble the trifles.

2 Slice the muffin, spread thinly with marmalade and arrange at the bottom of the dish, cutting as necessary to form a neat layer. Sprinkle with liqueur. Peel the mandarins and either slice into bite-size chunks, or if you prefer, segment them (see Trick of the Trade, page 168). Add these to the bowl along with the juice of the extra mandarin. Stir the jelly in its pot to break it up, microwave for 20–30 seconds to loosen it a little and spoon on top of the fruit. Refrigerate for 15 minutes, till set.

3 Spoon on the custard. Whip the remaining cream to soft peaks and blob or pile on top. Top with the candied marmalade shreds, if using. This dessert can be made a few hours ahead and chilled till you are ready to enjoy it.

Lemon lava pudding

My favourite nursery pudding – a delicate sponge with a surprise lemony sauce underneath – looks sweet baked in ovenproof cups or ramekins as 2 individual servings. It's not difficult to make, but produces a surprising amount of washing up. Serve warm from the oven, with chilled cream.

1 Lavishly butter 2 ovenproof dishes, each 250–300 ml/8½–10 fl oz. (generous 1–1¼ cup) capacity. Stand them in a roasting tin or pan or deep baking tray or sheet and put on the kettle. In a small food processor, whizz the butter, sugar and lemon zest till smooth, wiping down the sides as necessary with a spatula. One by one, whizz in the lemon juice, egg yolk, flour, milk and vanilla extract, to make a batter. Transfer to a medium bowl.

2 In a separate bowl, whisk the egg white to soft peaks and fold it into the lemon mixture till bouffant, and no blobs of egg white remain.

3 Divide the mixture between the prepared dishes and pour boiling water into the roasting tin, to ¼ or ⅓ of the height of the dishes. Carefully transfer the tin to the oven. Bake at 160°C fan/180°C/350°F for about 35 minutes, until the puddings are golden and slightly cracked.

4 The puddings will have miraculously set into a light sponge topping with a lemony sauce beneath. Leave for 5 minutes, dust with icing sugar and serve with chilled cream.

TRICK OF THE TRADE

*There can't be much to **squeezing a lemon**, can there? Well, to get the most juice out of it, give it a work-out first, by rolling it around on your countertop. This breaks down the membranes and means it will yield more juice.*

25 g/2 tbsp butter, plus extra
   for the dishes
50 g/1¾ oz./¼ cup caster/
   superfine sugar
finely grated zest and juice
   of ½ a lemon
1 egg, any size, separated
20 g/2⅓ tbsp self-raising/rising
   flour, or 20 g/2⅓ tbsp plain/
   all-purpose flour plus
   ¼ tsp baking powder
125 ml/4 fl oz./½ cup milk
a few drops of vanilla extract
a little icing/confectioners'
   sugar, to dust
double/heavy cream, to serve

New York cheesecake

There is nothing quite as delicious as home-made cheesecake, but most recipes use pounds of cream cheese, and are designed for parties and gatherings. For smaller households who want cheesecake in their lives, but not day after day after day, here is my favourite recipe, carefully reformulated to be baked in a small loaf tin or pan.

Loaf tin sizes are confusing (they're based on weights of bread dough, which is fine if you're a professional baker). For this recipe, you will need what is known as a '1-lb. loaf tin/pan' with a base of about 17 x 7 cm, 5 cm high, capacity 600 ml (typically a 1-lb. pan is 8 x 4 x 2 inches in the US).

FOR THE CRUST

3 digestives or shortbread
    biscuits/butter cookies
    (about 45 g/1½ oz.)
1 tbsp soft brown sugar
1 tbsp flour
a pinch of salt
15 g/1 tbsp butter, melted

FOR THE FILLING

1 egg, any size, beaten
2 tbsp soured cream
180 g/6¼ oz./¾ cup full-fat
    cream cheese, such as
    Philadelphia, softened
    (see Trick of the Trade)
3 tbsp caster/superfine sugar
2 tsp flour
½ tsp vanilla extract
finely grated zest of ¼ a lemon
½ tsp lemon juice

FOR THE TOPPING

3 tbsp soured cream
1 tsp sugar
½ tsp lemon juice
a few drops of vanilla extract

TO SERVE (OPTIONAL)

fresh berries, such as
    blueberries and raspberries
a little icing/confectioners'
    sugar, to dust

1 Line the loaf tin or pan by cutting 2 strips of foil, one to fit across, one lengthwise, with generous overhang to help to lift out the cheesecake once it's cooked. Grease the foil, or spray with non-stick spray.

2 Break the biscuits into the bowl of a small food processor with the sugar, flour and salt and pulse to form crumbs. Add the melted butter and pulse until just combined, like coarse, lumpy sand. Turn into the lined loaf tin and use a small palette knife to press the crumbs down in a compact, even layer. Bake at 140°C fan/160°C/325°F for about 12 minutes, until dry and lightly browned. Allow to cool while you make the filling.

3 Assemble all the filling ingredients before you start, and whisk the egg with the soured cream. Using a stand or hand mixer, beat the cream cheese and sugar until creamy – about 2 minutes – then gradually beat in the remaining ingredients. The batter should be smooth and light. Pour into the loaf tin and bake for about 25 minutes, by which time the top and edges should be set, but the centre should have a slight jiggle to it. (A cocktail stick inserted into the centre will not come out clean, but if you have a digital thermometer, the centre should read about 62°C/144°F.) Remove the cheesecake and leave to cool for at least 1½ hours – if a crack or cracks appear, no problem.

4 Lift the cheesecake out of the tin using the foil and put on a plate. Mix the topping ingredients, fold down the foil sides so they are not in the way and spread the topping over the top of the cheesecake, right to the edges. Refrigerate, uncovered, for 8 hours, or overnight.

5 Use a spatula to lift the cheesecake off its foil onto a plate. Cut into slices, add a few berries and dust with icing sugar, if liked, and serve.

TRICK OF THE TRADE

Cream cheese will not whip properly – and form lumps in the finished cheesecake – unless it is at room temperature. If you forget to get it out in advance, float the unopened tub or pack in hand-hot water for a few minutes before use.

Chocolate lava pudding

You can tell I love lava puddings. This one could not be more different from lemon lava pudding – intense, fudgy and utterly decadent. Under the chocolate crust is a pool of chocolate sauce.

To turn this into a delicious Mocha lava pudding, swap the boiling water in the sauce for strong, freshly brewed coffee.

1 Lavishly butter an ovenproof baking dish of about 500-ml/17 fl-oz. (generous 2-cup) capacity – I use a shallow dish about 20 cm/8 inches square. Melt the butter, chocolate and ½ the cocoa powder together in a medium jug/pitcher or bowl in the microwave and allow to cool slightly. Whisk in the sugar, milk, egg yolk and vanilla, then the flour and a pinch of salt. Transfer to the prepared dish.

2 Mix the topping ingredients in a small bowl with a fork, and sprinkle evenly over the pudding. Finally, carefully pour the boiling water gently over the top.

3 Bake this unpromising mixture at 140°C fan/160°C/325°F for about 35 minutes, until the pudding is firm in places, and gently bubbling. Leave for 5 minutes, dust lightly with cocoa powder, if liked, then serve with cream, because, why not?

TRICK OF THE TRADE

*I know from experience that many a cook gets hot under the collar with regard to plain and **self-raising/rising flour**. I keep both in my storecupboard, purely for convenience, but you can convert plain to self-raising by whisking 100 g/3½ oz./¾ cup plain/all-purpose flour with 1 teaspoon baking powder. It's that simple – but don't use bicarbonate of soda/baking soda by mistake.*

*While talking flour, scientific experiments have shown that **whisking and sifting** flour achieve the same thing. By all means sift flour if you wish – hold the sieve/ strainer high over the bowl if you want to get flour over the entire kitchen – but a quick whisk in the bowl does the same job, believe me.*

25 g/2 tbsp butter, plus extra
 for the dish
20 g/¾ oz. dark/bittersweet
 chocolate, chopped
4 tsp cocoa powder
4 tsp sugar
2 tbsp milk
1 egg yolk, any size
1 tsp vanilla extract
25 g/3 tbsp self-raising/rising
 flour, or 25 g/3 tbsp plain/
 all-purpose flour plus ¼ tsp
 baking powder
 (see Trick of the Trade)
a pinch of salt

FOR THE TOPPING
3 tbsp soft brown sugar
1 tbsp caster/superfine sugar
4 tsp cocoa powder, plus a little
 extra to finish

FOR THE SAUCE
120 ml/4 fl oz./½ cup boiling
 water, or a mixture of boiling
 water and coffee
 (see recipe introduction)
double/heavy cream, or whipped
 cream, to serve

Passion possets with shortbread of love

Many years ago when I edited BBC Good Food magazine, I remember food director Mary Cadogan rushing into my office, eyes bright with excitement. She was trying out an ancient recipe and made an amazing discovery. If you boil double cream and sugar for a few minutes, then stir in citrus juice, it sets into a beautiful silky custard – known as a posset. Ridiculously easy – sublimely delicious. Take your time over this elegant recipe, to allow the posset and jelly to set. For a special or romantic occasion, it can be further fancied with a home-made shortbread.

2 passionfruit
3–4 clementines or satsumas
150 ml/5 fl oz./²⁄₃ cup double
    cream, or 180 ml/6 fl oz./
    ¾ cup heavy or whipping
    cream (in the US)
30 g/1 oz./2½ tbsp white sugar
juice of ¼ a lemon

FOR THE JELLY
1 gelatin sheet, or ½ tsp gelatin
    powder
1 tsp sugar

FOR THE CLEMENTINE
SHORTBREAD (OPTIONAL)
(makes about 15)
3 tbsp caster/superfine sugar
1 tbsp light/soft brown sugar
85 g/6 tbsp butter, softened
finely grated zest of
    ½ a clementine
1 tsp vanilla extract
2 tsp egg yolk (10 g/¹⁄₃ oz.)
110 g/4 oz./¾ cup plus 1½ tbsp
    flour
an extra clementine, peeled and
    segmented, to serve (see
    Trick of the Trade, page 168)
    (optional)
a little icing/confectioners'
    sugar, to dust

1 Halve the passionfruit and scoop the flesh into a small sieve/strainer set over a small bowl. Use a spoon or small ladle (easier) to press out as much juice as you can into a small measuring jug/pitcher. Discard the gunk in the sieve. Squeeze in the clementines – stop when you have a total of 125 ml/4 fl oz. (½ cup) juice, and set aside.

2 Bring the cream and sugar to the boil in a medium saucepan – to allow room for the cream to bubble up – and keep bubbling for 3 minutes, whisking constantly. For heavy or whipping cream, which is lower in fat content than British double cream, increase the time to 3½ minutes. (If you wish, you can check you have reduced the cream sufficiently by transferring it to a measuring jug – it should measure 100–120 ml/3¹⁄₃–4 fl oz. (generous ¹⁄₃–½ cup).

3 Stir in 2 tablespoons of the passionfruit-clementine mixture and the lemon juice, leave for 3–5 minutes, then pour into 2 small glasses (each about 125-ml/4 fl-oz. (½-cup) capacity and put in the fridge for 3 hours, till set.

4 Next, the jelly topping. If using sheet gelatin, put it in a wide dish, cover with cold water and leave for 4 minutes. Meanwhile, warm the reserved passionfruit-clementine mixture to hand-hot. Lift out the gelatine, squeeze lightly to drain and stir into the passionfruit mixture till dissolved. Cool completely, then pour over the cold-set posset. If using powder, heat 1 tablespoon of passionfruit mixture, in a small bowl, in the microwave, sprinkle over the gelatine and stir to dissolve completely. Stir this into the remaining passionfruit mixture. (If the mixture looks at all granular, you haven't dissolved the gelatine properly, so heat the mixture to hand-hot and stir till clear.) Cool and pour over the cold, set posset. Put in the fridge and leave for 3–24 hours, covering with plastic film once the jelly is set.

5 *For the clementine shortbread* (if making), whizz the sugars and zest together in a small food processor. Add the butter, vanilla and egg yolk

and whizz again. Scraping down the processor sides as necessary, add the flour and whizz till a soft dough forms. Wrap in plastic wrap and chill. Line a baking tray or sheet with baking parchment. Roll the chilled dough out to a thickness of 5–8 mm/¼–⅜ inch and stamp out shapes. Arrange on the baking tray and bake at 160°C fan/180°C/350°F for 13–15 minutes, till the edges are pale gold. Leave to cool, then dust with icing sugar.

7 Segment the remaining clementine, if using (see Trick of the Trade, below). Beautify each posset with clementine segments and a shortbread, if liked, and take a bow.

TRICK OF THE TRADE

Segmenting citrus *into neat crescents, free of pith, skin and membrane is easy once you know how. Having spent ten years as a chef whose first job every morning was to make fresh fruit salad, I am in a position to explain how it's done. Peel the outside of a citrus of all skin, pith and membrane using a small sharp knife. Lay the fruit on its side and rotate until you find a clearly defined segment. Slice down one side of the segment (leaving the membrane behind) then the other, and wiggle the segment out. The first is always hardest. Now proceed with one of the adjacent segments, and so on, turning the fruit as you go. You will be left with a shell of membrane to discard, and a pile of bright and juicy segments. It may seem a lot of trouble for a tiny result, but for this elegant recipe, and a special occasion, it's well worth it.*

Birthday surprise

This decadent creation, with its vertical stripes, is a sort of Swiss roll turned on end. It draws inspiration from a lemon and blackcurrant spiral cake invented by Yotam Ottolenghi and Helen Goh. Making cakes is something that many two-person households miss out on; a normal size cake is too big, so you either end up eating too much of it, or throwing some away. Here, I have reduced quantities to the absolute minimum that a normal food mixer can handle. You can use a hand mixer, but prepare yourself for almost 15 minutes of whisking.

1 For the cake, you either need an 18 x 33-cm/7 x 13-inch tin or pan, lined with baking parchment, or you can fashion one out of baking parchment (or better still, foil-lined baking parchment). To do this, fold up the sides and ends of the parchment to measure 18 x 33 cm/7 x 13 inches, place in a shallow baking tin or pan (mine measures 23 x 33 cm/9 x 13 inches, which helps support each end). Staple the corners to improve stability.

2 Put the egg yolks in the mixer bowl and start off with the paddle attachment, which tends to reach the bottom of the bowl better. Beat for 5 minutes, scraping down the sides occasionally. Change to the whisk attachment and trickle in the water mixed with the extracts, then the sugar, spoonful by spoonful. Whisk on for 5 minutes, by which time it should be beginning to thicken slightly, look pale and moussey and leave a faint trail when the whisk is lifted.

3 Whisk the flour, cornflour, baking powder and salt in a small bowl. In another, whisk the egg whites to soft peaks. Sprinkle the flour over the yolk mixture, fold in with a rubber spatula, then fold in ⅓ of the egg whites, then the rest. Transfer to the lined baking tin, or your hand-made equivalent and smooth with a spatula. Bake at 160°C fan/180°C/350°F for 18–20 minutes, until risen, pale gold and spongy (not squishy) to the touch. Allow to cool for 4 minutes, then invert onto a fresh piece of baking parchment on a board. Peel the top parchment away delicately (make sure you don't leave any staples behind), then use a pizza wheel or knife to straighten each long side and slice down the centre, to form 2 strips, about 9 x 33 cm/3½ x 13 inches. Roll both strips up tightly (including the parchment), and leave to cool completely for at least 30 minutes, so the cake 'sets' in the right shape.

4 Melt the 75 g/2¾ oz. chocolate – about 2 minutes in the microwave at 50% power – and transfer to a small plastic bag. Whip the cream with the sugar and vanilla to soft peaks. Carefully unroll the cake. Reposition 1 of the strips at the end of the other, so you have one narrow strip of cake about 66 cm/26 inches long. Sprinkle lightly with brandy, if using.

FOR THE CAKE
2 eggs, any size, separated
50 ml/1⅔ fl. oz/3½ tbsp water
¼ tsp each vanilla and almond extracts
120 g/4½ oz./⅔ cup minus 1 tsp caster/superfine sugar
80 g/2¾ oz./⅔ cup minus 1 tbsp flour
4 tsp cornflour/cornstarch
¼ tsp baking powder
a pinch of salt

FOR THE FILLING
75 g/2¾ oz. dark/bittersweet chocolate
150 ml/5 fl oz./⅔ cup double/heavy cream
1 tbsp sugar
1 tsp vanilla extract
2–3 tbsp brandy, or liqueur of your choice (optional)
3 tbsp raspberry jam/preserve (seedless or strained, beaten)

FOR THE FROSTING
70 g/2½ oz. dark/bittersweet chocolate, melted and cooled
80 g/6 tbsp butter, softened (see Trick of the Trade, page 70)
4 tbsp icing/confectioners' sugar, sifted, plus extra to dust
2 tbsp cocoa powder, sifted
1 tbsp maple or golden syrup
½ tsp vanilla extract
a few fresh berries and edible gold leaf flakes, to decorate

TRICK OF THE TRADE

*The French for **softened butter** is 'pommade' (literally, ointment). When this is specified in a recipe, it needs to be completely soft – almost melted – and if your kitchen is on the cool side, it will need to be warmed. You can speed things up by chopping the butter up, or you can microwave in 10-second increments, or both. If you go too far and the butter starts to melt around the edges, it can still be used. If you melt it fully by mistake – believe me on this – stir in an ice cube or two to re-firm the butter (and then throw away the semi-melted ice).*

Spread with the jam, right to the edges, then the whipped cream. Snip the corner of the chocolate bag and flick the chocolate all over the cream in thin zigzags. This will set to form a crunchy texture. Roll the cake up tightly from one short end, keeping it as neat as you can, then up-end onto a serving plate. Neaten the shape with your hands – if it seems to want to unroll, swaddle it with plastic film to hold in shape. Refrigerate.

5 Make the frosting by beating all the ingredients till smooth. Spread around the side of the cake (slide little strips of parchment under the bottom edge to keep the plate clean), then the top. Leave for 1 hour to set, then refrigerate for up to 12 hours. Chilling can make the frosting go dull, but its sheen can be restored by gently blow drying, from a distance of about 50 cm/20 inches (don't overdo this). Top with berries and flakes of gold leaf, dust with icing sugar and adorn with candles, if you wish. To serve, slice with a thin serrated knife, used in a gentle sawing motion.

Index

TRICKS OF THE TRADE

Acknowledgements

My first thanks must go to my fellow cooks and food writers, from whose vast experience I have learnt more than I could possibly have done in a dozen lifetimes. My style of cooking has been shaped by two main resources – BBC Good Food in the UK, and Cooks' Illustrated in the United States. I ride on the shoulders of their rigorous testing and investigative excellence – and more recently, the work of Serious Eats.

Whenever in doubt, I consult my online oracles, Delia Smith and Felicity Cloake, and find myself in perpetual awe of their creativity, inventiveness and diligence. During my career in the magazine world, I had the good fortune to witness some of the all-time great food writers at work, including Mary Cadogan, Angela Nilsen, Sara Buenfeld, Barney Desmazery and Cassie Best. If my recipes work in your kitchen, as I sincerely hope they will, this is a skill I largely learnt from these great recipe writers.

I hope you will find everything on these pages practical and realistic, and I have tried to include the widest possible range of recipes, to open your eyes to what it is possible to achieve on a small scale. But let this be just the beginning. I urge you always to be open to culinary adventures – to trying something new – and travel to the unknown. I was deliciously reminded of how fun and exciting this can be when, shortly before starting work on this book, I picked up Marlena Spieler's *A Taste of Naples*, and decided to make her *Lasagna Napoletana o Carnevalesca*. This sumptuous recipe positively reeked of authenticity, and covered three pages: the first step was to make the sausages. Oh what an adventure! Allow yourself to be transported by authentic cooking, from authentic cooks, with stories and heritage to share from around the world. Dorie Greenspan, Rachel Roddy, Jill Dupleix, Paula Wolfert, Tessa Kiros, Yotam Ottolenghi, Alice Waters, Judy Rodgers – all these and many other 'authentic' food writers have served as magic carpets in my culinary life.

In compiling this book, I have encountered the odd frustration, when I collided with a recipe-for-two that someone else wrote, and simply cannot be improved upon. Nigel Slater, in particular, often seems to have got there first.

I have the honour to be President of that august association known as The Guild of Food Writers, which represents and provides a community for the UK's professional writers and broadcasters. I am grateful for the help, friendship and support I gain from it, most notably from Mallika Basu, an unrivalled expert in the fields of 'diversity', authenticity and recipe appropriation. Other influencers from within the Guild – either by their approach, recipes or assistance – include my podcast companions Tom Kerridge and Rosie Birkett, Xanthe Clay, Charlotte Pike, Ruth Watson, Di Murrell, Jeni Wright, Elaine Boddy, Meera Sodha, Helen-Best Shaw, Ruth Nieman, Nellie Nichols and Dawn Stock.

Twelve years ago, on a food writing course, I made six special friends: we meet up each year, and there is always much to celebrate. They are Pauline Beaumont, Kristen Frederickson, Samuel Goldsmith, Rosie 'Foxie' Jones, Katie Socker and Susan Willis. Pauline's *Bread Therapy* and Kristen's *Tonight at 7.30* and sequel *Second Helpings* are on the bookshelf in front of me, along with food mags edited by Sam and novels by Susan.

I would also like to thank my friend and sounding-board Barbara Baker and my kind neighbour Amy Shelton and her son Laurie (for dummy-running a couple of recipes, and their enthusiastic welcome of surplus ingredients). Farnaz Massoumian, for a lifetime supply of saffron. Janet East, whose universal expertize includes butchery. At the very start of this project, my friend Mary Forde told me what she would hope for from a book like this, and I have borne her insightful words in mind throughout all my experiments and testing.

I suspect some authors thank their agents and publishers through gritted teeth, but that is the opposite of the truth in this case. Without my agent, publishing doyenne Heather Holden-Brown, this book would not be in your hands now. She is the agent of one's dreams, and I'd like to thank her for the fun we have had, as well as her perspicacity and persistence. And Elly James at HHB, too, for her sharp eye and mind. The team at Ryland Peters & Small has been – from the very outset – a joy to work with. Thank you to Cindy Richards for believing in the project, and Julia Charles for your inspirational guidance and masterful editing. I have no idea how the design and shoot team can have made my recipes look so beautiful, but thank you Leslie Harrington, Megan Smith, Polly Webb-Wilson, Tamara Vos and Clare Winfield for doing so.

At a domestic level, infinite thanks to Robert for putting up with months of testing and retesting, plus occasional fits of despair or hysterics, with patience and good humour. And our feline family, Nola – very much missed – and now the two boy cats, Benjamin and Maxim, for the fun, love and joy they bring to our household.